RELIGION, CU

Reflections on the

The principle of reasonable accommodation requires that the cultural majority make certain concessions to the needs of minority groups if these concessions will not cause 'undue hardship.' This principle has caused much debate in Québec, particularly over issues of language, Muslim head coverings, and religious symbols such as the kirpan (traditional Sikh dagger). In 2007, Québec Premier Jean Charest commissioned historian and sociologist Gérard Bouchard and philosopher and political scientist Charles Taylor to co-chair a commission that would investigate the limits of reasonable accommodation in that province.

Religion, Culture, and the State addresses reasonable accommodation from legal, political, and anthropological perspectives. Using the 2008 Bouchard-Taylor Report as their point of departure, the contributors to this volume examine the English and French Canadian experiences of multiculturalism and diversity through socio-historical assessment and comparative analysis focusing on France, the United Kingdom, and the United States. Timely and engaging, *Religion, Culture, and the State* is a valuable addition to the literature on religious pluralism in Canadian society.

HOWARD ADELMAN is a professor emeritus at York University.

PIERRE ANCTIL is a professor in the Department of History at the University of Ottawa.

EDITED BY HOWARD ADELMAN
AND PIERRE ANCTIL

Religion, Culture, and the State

Reflections on the Bouchard-Taylor Report

UNIVERSITY OF TORONTO PRESS
Toronto Buffalo London

©University of Toronto Press Incorporated 2011
Toronto Buffalo London
www.utppublishing.com
Printed in Canada

ISBN 978-1-4426-4261-4 (cloth)
ISBN 978-1-4426-1144-3 (paper)

Printed on acid-free, 100% post-consumer recycled paper with vegetable-based inks.

Library and Archives Canada Cataloguing in Publication

Religion, culture, and the state: reflections on the Bouchard-Taylor report / edited by Howard Adelman and Pierre Anctil.

Includes bibliographical references.
ISBN 978-1-4426-4261-4 (bound). – ISBN 978-1-4426-1144-3 (pbk.)

1. Religious pluralism – Canada   2. Religious pluralism – Québec (Province).   3. Cultural pluralism – Canada.   4. Cultural pluralism – Québec (Province).   5. Québec (Province) – Ethnic relations.   6. Multiculturalism – Canada.   7. Multiculturalism – Québec (Province).
I. Adelman, Howard, 1938–   II. Anctil, Pierre, 1952–

BL2530.C3R45 2011   201'.50971   C2011-901196-4

University of Toronto Press acknowledges the financial assistance to its publishing program of the Canada Council for the Arts and the Ontario Arts Council.

 Canada Council Conseil des Arts
for the Arts du Canada

 ONTARIO ARTS COUNCIL
CONSEIL DES ARTS DE L'ONTARIO

University of Toronto Press acknowledges the financial support of the Government of Canada through the Canada Book Fund for its publishing activities.

This book is dedicated to Ralph Halbert, the principal donor and dedicated Canadian who founded the Halbert Centre for Canadian Studies at the Hebrew University of Jerusalem

The Halbert Centre for Canadian Studies supports and funds research on Canada by researchers and graduate students at the Hebrew University of Jerusalem.

Contents

Contributors ix

Introduction 3
PIERRE ANCTIL

1 Reasonable Accommodation in the Canadian Legal Context:
  A Mechanism for Handling Diversity or a Source of Tension? 16
  PIERRE ANCTIL

2 Monoculturalism versus Interculturalism
  in a Multicultural World. 37
  HOWARD ADELMAN

3 The Bouchard-Taylor Commission and the Jewish Community
  of Québec in Historical Perspective 58
  IRA ROBINSON

4 'Qui est nous?' Some Answers from the Bouchard-Taylor
  Commission's Archive 69
  BINA TOLEDO FREIWALD

5 The B-T Report 'Open Secularism' Model and the Supreme Court
  of Canada Decisions on Freedom of Religion and Religious
  Accommodation 86
  JOSÉ WOEHRLING

6 Conclusion: Religion, Culture, and the State 100
  HOWARD ADELMAN

Notes 117

References 141

Contributors

Howard Adelman recently completed a three-year term as research professor at the Key Centre for Ethics, Law, Justice and Governance at Griffith University in Brisbane, Australia. Previously, he was a visiting professor at the Woodrow Wilson School at Princeton University, and from 1966 to 2003 was a professor of philosophy at York University in Toronto where he founded and was the first director of the Centre for Refugee Studies and editor of *Refuge* until the end of 1993. He has written or co-authored 10 books, and edited or co-edited 21 others. He has authored 75 chapters in edited volumes, 97 articles in refereed journals, and 31 professional reports. In addition to his numerous writings on refugees, he has written articles, chapters, and books on the Middle East, multiculturalism, humanitarian intervention, membership rights, ethics, and early warning and conflict management. His edited volume, *Protracted Displacement in Asia: No Place to Call Home*, was released in November 2008 by Ashgate. Professor Adelman recently completed a co-authored book with Elazar Barkan entitled *Rites of Return* for Columbia University Press.

Pierre Anctil was the director of the Institute of Canadian Studies at the University of Ottawa until July 2008. Before that date, he was president of the Conseil des relations interculturelles of the Government of Québec (2002–2003), and has held different positions in the Québec civil service in the domain of immigration (1991– 2004). He was a guest researcher (1999–2000) at Musée Pointe-à-Callière for the conception of an exhibit on boulevard Saint-Laurent (2002), and for an international exhibition on the Bible and the Dead Sea Scrolls (2003). He was also director of the French Canadian Studies Program at McGill University

(1988–1991) and researcher at the Institut québécois de recherche sur la culture (1980–1988). He was adjunct professor at the Department of History of the Université du Québec à Montréal (1996–2004) and a member of the Institut québécois d'études sur la culture juive (1987–2006). He has written at length on the history of the Jewish community of Montréal and on the current debates on cultural pluralism in Montréal. Among his contributions are translations, from Yiddish to French, of memoirs written by Jewish immigrants to Montréal in the first half of the twentieth century. For the period 2008–2010, he was awarded a Killam fellowship by the Canada Council for the Arts for research entitled 'Parcours migrant, parcours littéraire canadien, le poète yiddish Jacob-Isaac Segal.' His latest book, *trajectoires juives au Québec*, was published by les Presses de l'Université Laval in 2010.

Bina Toledo Freiwald is professor of English and director of the Humanities PhD Program (Centre for Interdisciplinary Studies in Society and Culture) at Concordia University in Montreal. Her areas of teaching and research include critical theory, Canadian literature, contemporary women's writing across genres and national literatures, autobiographical practices, and identity discourses. Recent publications include chapters in *Wider Boundaries of Daring: The Modernist Impulse in Canadian Women's Poetry* (2009); *Unfitting Stories: Narrative Approaches to Disease, Disability, and Trauma* (2007); the Norton Critical Edition of Susanna Moodie's *Roughing It in the Bush* (2007); *Tracing the Autobiographical* (2005); *Postmodernism and the Ethical Subject* (2004); and *Identity, Community, Nation: Essays on Canadian Writing* (2002). Her current research project is 'Gender, Nation, and Self-Narration: The Construction of National and Diasporic Identities in Jewish Women's Life Narratives in Palestine/*Eretz Israel* and Canada 1880–1948.'

Ira Robinson is professor of Judaic Studies in the Department of Religion, Concordia University, Montreal. He is currently president of the Canadian Society for Jewish Studies and is the former president of the Association for Canadian Jewish Studies and the Jewish Public Library (Montreal). His latest book is *Translating a Tradition: Studies in American Jewish History* (2008).

José Woehrling teaches Canadian and comparative constitutional law at the Faculty of Law at the Université de Montréal. He has published extensively on federalism, human rights, and minority protection in

Canada as well as abroad. In past decades, he has been asked to give expert opinion and advice in the context of some of the most important constitutional and political developments in Québec, such as the two referenda on sovereignty-association; the Bélanger-Campeau Commission; the failed Meech Lake and Charlottetown constitutional packages; Québec's language policy and the legal challenges against the Charter of the French Language; the bilateral constitutional amendment of Section 93 of the Constitution Act of 1867 in its application to Québec, and the ensuing reorganization of the provincial school system; the position of the Québec government on Senate and Supreme Court reform; and the controversy about religious accommodation and the Bouchard-Taylor Commission. He has been a visiting professor to universities in Belgium, Switzerland, Germany, France, Italy, Spain, and Australia.

RELIGION, CULTURE, AND THE STATE

Reflections on the Bouchard-Taylor Report

Introduction

PIERRE ANCTIL

The objective of this book is to explore the issue of religious pluralism in Canadian society, particularly in Québec, as it has emerged in the last decade.[1] Canada has a strong reputation around the world for its tolerance of diversity and its multicultural policies as they apply to recently arrived immigrant communities. At various levels of government, several legal instruments have been put in place to protect the rights of linguistic minorities and the basic freedoms of individuals. Nonetheless, new challenges have arisen in our society that touch upon the public display of religious symbols and the need to accommodate rituals and spiritual beliefs not previously visible in Canada. Although the Charter of Rights and Freedoms, which specifically covers the right to freedom of conscience and religion, was approved by the Canadian Parliament in 1982, few guidelines exist, other than those provided by the courts, to deal with the ever-increasing religious diversity that affects the workplace, the delivery of services by governments, and the administration of justice. This difficult situation has been dramatically highlighted by the influx of immigrants to Canada from several regions of the world, where Christianity is at best a minority practice and where public authorities often enforce legal codes of conduct derived directly from non-Christian, fundamentalist religious traditions. While multiculturalism and official language legislation were designed in the sixties and seventies to answer tensions arising from the coexistence in the country of minorities (in the linguistic or racial sense of the term), currently they offer very little help with regard to the multiplicity of non-Western religious beliefs on display in all major Canadian cities.

In the belief that a very detailed exploration of particular issues, contexts, and processes may be the best way to understand a worldwide problem, this collection of essays focuses more precisely on the issue of religious diversity in the context of Québec society as explored in the hearings and report of the Consultation Commission on Accommodation Practices,[2] held in 2007–8 under the co-chairmanship of Gérard Bouchard[3] and Charles Taylor.[4] Unlike any other province, Québec has designed its own official policy with regard to cultural pluralism, called 'interculturalism,' and has been witness in the last few years to an intense public debate centred on the integration of recent immigrants in the French language institutions and schools of the province. Because the vast majority of the francophone population in Québec during the Quiet Revolution (1960 to 1966) rejected the influence of the then-dominant Catholic Church, the resurgence of spiritual beliefs in public affairs has sparked a strong reaction, in part influenced by the French republican concept of *laïcité*. Moreover, after creating a provincial ministry of immigration in 1968 for the purpose of addressing the international flow of immigrants within its own borders, Québec directly administers several programs designed to facilitate the integration of newcomers, and maintains a wide range of specialized health and social services for this clientele.

While multiculturalism is used at the federal level to 'promote the full and equitable participation of individuals and communities of all origins in the continuing evolution and shaping of all aspects of Canadian society,'[5] Québec simultaneously developed a similar approach under the distinct heading of interculturalism. Since multiculturalism is language-blind, and in its programs do not take into account the issue of Canada's official languages, the main difference between the two notions has been the necessity in Québec society of integrating immigrants in the French language. From this perspective, interculturalism does not contradict the stated multicultural ideology used elsewhere in Canada, as is evidenced by the definition of the term provided by the Québec Ministry of Immigration and Cultural Communities: 'Québec, which is attuned to interculturalism, takes full advantage of the social, political, cultural and economic wealth derived from its acceptation of pluralism, of diversity and of the multiplicity of origins.'[6]

In recent years, this broad preoccupation with cultural plurality culminated in a series of events which were widely publicized in the Montreal press and found their way into the wider media on an almost daily basis. Perhaps, because of its unique political culture and history, Québécois society seemed to be out of tempo with the more sedate approach to pluralism found in anglophone Canada; Québec directly confronted the major fundamental issues that were also evident elsewhere in the country. Could it be that Québec offered a markedly different type of answer to the emergence of religious pluralism, one that was more decidedly interventionist on the part of public authorities, while relying at the same time on a more radical separation of church and state? Was Québec proposing an avenue which, although based on the same general notions of human rights and freedoms, reflected its own distinctiveness within the Canadian ensemble? Or did the rooted cosmopolitanism that philosophers like Will Kymlicka espoused as characterizing the Canadian ethos serve as a cover for inherent contradictions in the Canadian system of dealing with minorities, particularly religious minorities (Kymlicka 1995b, 2001)? Are there interesting conclusions to be drawn from the Québec experience, itself the home of the largest linguistic minority in the country, and Canada's unique articulation of the way to deal with minorities? As Adam Gopnik (2009b: 30) wrote, '[T]he belief that the rights of the community can trump the rights of the individual – and that this is not incompatible with liberalism but exactly what humanizes it -- really is a distinctly Canadian intuition. It is argued in different ways, and with different emphasis, by the influential McGill philosopher Charles Taylor ... and by the essayist John Ralston Saul, and Queen's University philosopher Will Kymlicka.'[7]

* * *

In this explosive context, Jean Charest, the premier of Québec, announced in February 2007 that a commission would be formed with the purpose of clarifying the notion of *accommodement raisonnable* among the population in general. Named Commission de consultation sur les pratiques d'accommodement reliées aux differences culturelles,[8] it was to be headed by two well-recognized intellectuals, Gérard Bouchard and Charles Taylor. The creation of the Commission followed a series of incidents and misunderstandings widely reported in the francophone press during the course of 2006 and even earlier, which included the wearing of a hijāb by a girl while playing soccer, requests for places of worship within certain public facilities, the wearing of a kirpan by a young Sikh in a public school, the separation of men and women in public swimming places, and whether a YMCA near Outremont should grant the request of a neighbouring Hasidic community to shield its windows from outside view because supposedly scantily clad women could be seen by the Hasidic boys next door. Meanwhile, the leader of the Action démocratique du Québec, Mario Dumont, was clearly positioning himself as an opponent of the so-called concessions made to the cultural and religious minorities, and as the defender of the historical identity of the francophone majority within Québec. On several occasions in 2005 and 2006, Dumont, the leader of a right-wing and populist party, systematically attacked the provincial Liberals on their handling of ethnic diversity and underlined the growing uneasiness within the population with regard to the 'special privileges' offered minorities by official agencies. This campaign was widely seen by commentators as having the potential of successfully boosting the political profile of the young leader and positioning him favourably for the following provincial elections. The last straw came in January 2007 when the municipal council of Hérouxville, a small municipality north of Trois-Rivières, unilaterally passed a code of conduct directed at future immigrants which specified that no adjustments would be made for religious minorities and that accommodations reached elsewhere or under other jurisdictions would be rejected wholeheartedly. Ironically, Hérouxville, a small town with a population of 1,300 persons, had no visible minorities and had virtually no prospect of attracting newcomers in the near future.

As publicly announced, the Commission was mandated to take stock of existing practices with respect to diversity within Québec society, examine the issue elsewhere to better understand its long-term implications, and conduct a broad process of consultation reaching all classes of society. Finally, Bouchard and Taylor were to propose recommendations to the government to make sure that solutions already found and others to be implemented conformed to the core values of Québec as a pluralistic, democratic, and egalitarian society. This meant that the Commission could go beyond the strictly legal interpretations and court rulings already advanced, and could venture into all forms of arrangements, adjustments, and practices in place at all levels. This included wide-ranging consultations in all regions of Québec, where citizens would be allowed to speak freely on the issue and where all opinions could be voiced. In fact, more than 900 briefs were sent to the Commission and thousands of people attended the forums, where spontaneous interventions were permitted. These public events were televised and aroused considerable interest for several months, while Bouchard and Taylor literally toured the province and reached even areas where immigration was not a current issue and would probably not be in the foreseeable future.

Ironically, the notion of *accommodement raisonnable* (reasonable accommodation), which is at the root of the debate in Québec society, is in itself a fleeting notion which was largely misunderstood by the media and most of the citizens who addressed the Bouchard-Taylor Commission, not to mention several political figures who commented on the debate. In the French language, the term *accommodement* is widely used to describe a situation when two parties come to an agreement on how to resolve an issue at hand that is potentially divisive. Essentially it means using compromise and goodwill to negotiate a position that is respectful of the cultural and religious sensitivities of all involved. This is the reason why, in the last few years, virtually every potentially tense situation became a public issue and was reported as an example of the direction in which accommodement raisonnable could lead Québec society in general. The best example of this is the way the YMCA on avenue du Parc in Montreal came to an understanding with the Satmar Hasidic community, from which it was separated only by a back alley. In 2006, without any intervention from outside and after discussions with the Hasidim, the board of directors of the YMCA agreed to install windowpanes that would hide from the outside the normal activities taking place in their gym. Neither the courts nor the City of Montreal, which funds the YMCA, nor any other institution or body, were consulted in the process nor intervened to impose a solution. The *accommodement* backfired only when some users of the YMCA complained that the decision reached by the board of the institution violated the principle of laïcité supposedly common to all Québécois citizens. A petition was signed to reinstall the type of windowpanes previously in place. The controversy reached the media very quickly, and the affair became something of a *cause célèbre*. Eventually, in the eyes of many of the opponents to diversity, the issue symbolized how francophone Québec was giving up too much ground to religious minorities and abandoning the basic principles of its majority culture.

Our discussion opens with a chapter by myself, followed by a chapter by Howard Adelman of the Department of Philosophy at York University. Together they form a kind of dialogue on the way diversity is perceived and understood in France, in Canada, and in Québec. There is no doubt that each of these societies upholds democratic values and has its own charter of rights. In the case of Québec, a Charte des droits et libertés de la personne passed six years before the Canadian Charter of Rights and Freedoms. Because of historical factors and deep-seated cultural perceptions, specific applications of the overarching principles described above do tend to vary considerably. For instance, decisions taken in France regarding the wearing of the hijāb by young Muslim women in public schools would have been judged unconstitutional in both Quebec and the rest of Canada (ROC), the banning of headgear in France an outward sign of faith being contrary, in this country, to the basic freedom of religion.

This is all the more interesting, since initially few outside observers would be tempted to view the strict application of the principle of laïcité in France as a violation of human rights legislation, all the more since it was conceived in the first place in the aftermath of the French Revolution as a tool to remove inequalities and keep the traditional influence of the Catholic Church at bay. Perhaps, after all, there are different and nonetheless acceptable readings and interpretations of the fundamental rights of citizens. In France, for example, defenders of laïcité and of a strict reading of the values of republicanism criticize multiculturalism and *communautarisme* as a slippery slope leading to unacceptable inequity between citizens. In other words, from a French point of view, as soon as the state begins to make distinctions based on colour, country of origin, ethnicity, or religion, sometimes assuming the role of an arbiter between minorities and the majority, which is exactly what the ideology of multiculturalism proposes, then, in the dominant French view, this path opens the gates to privileges, and encourages the appearance of special classes of citizens.

In a country where there is no tolerance whatsoever for a multicultural vision of society, such as France, the Canadian perspective tends to appear as rather unwise politically and unnecessarily divisive. Often it is forgotten in this perspective that Canada is not a centralized state and that many cultural communities converged to form the country, notably the First Nations and recently a host of very divergent immigrant groups. Likewise, to the advocates of a federal brand of Canadian multiculturalism and for those who pursue a race relations agenda, the Québec ideology of interculturalism appears ineffective and sometimes even contradictory to its own objectives. Why would there be a need in the Québécois sphere of responsibility for a separate and somewhat competing set of values from those generally accepted in Canada? Is the use of interculturalism in the provincial domains of immigration and school integration, and in the perception of cultural diversity, not adding confusion to an already complex issue rather than simplifying it? Clearly Bouchard and Taylor sided with interculturalism and reaffirmed the uniqueness of Québec society, its achievements in welcoming newcomers, and its political autonomy in the internal definition of pluralism. In other words, for the Commission and for many of the citizens who expressed their opinion in public fora, a truly separate path for Québec required unique measures and an ideology different from the pan-Canadian one. Is this acceptable and tolerable in a vast country like Canada? Will interculturalism be more effective or less than its federal counterpart? Is francophone Québec inherently biased in its approach to diversity or is it more creative and open-minded? To many who argued before the Bouchard-Taylor Commission, the fact that a cultural identity in Québec exists in a different form from the rest of Canada is sufficient to justify interculturalism. Others presented the view that multiculturalism is language-blind, and that left to its own devices would clearly encourage the integration of immigrants into the anglophone stream, thus weakening the prospects for the survival of francophone culture in Québec. Knowing how sensitive the language debate is in Montreal, this position carried a great deal of weight in the recent past.

Beyond the historical and philosophical considerations discussed by the two authors who also edited this collection, the issue at hand also has important ramifications in the narrower domain of law. The contribution by José Woehrling, a professor in the Faculty of Law at the Université de Montréal, attempts to situate the debate in the legal sphere in light of the advances made since the passing of the Canadian Charter of Rights and Freedoms in 1982. Reasonable accommodation is essentially a legal concept which appeared when federal courts judged that the provisions designed to protect various minorities from discrimination could miss their targets, especially in the case of certain groups who were victims of a long history of marginality and vulnerability within Canadian society. For this reason, courts tended to go beyond the notion of abstract equality and to propose specific measures to ensure that the general result sought by the Charter was reached more efficiently, even to the point of proposing specific and limited accommodations or remedies adapted to well-defined cases. In chapter 5 Woehrling discusses several examples of federal court rulings that attempted to protect the religious beliefs of private citizens confronted with legal obstacles, to the point of being denied their basic rights in the religious sphere. Sadly, this distinction between open-ended negotiations without legal significance, as in the case of the avenue du Parc YMCA, and court rulings touching very precise circumstances of discrimination and marginalization, was missed by most commentators in the public sphere. Likewise, Woehrling presents a discussion on the choices made by the Commission with regard to laïcité, and how this notion was interpreted by the opponents of religious tolerance. Because the example of France and its republican principles are often cited in Québec society, many of the briefs submitted to Bouchard and Taylor proposed a rigid interpretation of the neutrality of the state vis-à-vis religion, which runs contrary to the legal foundations in the Constitution of Canada and in the British parliamentary tradition in general. This confrontation of two distinct modes of thought will likely become a dominant trait within Québec society in the near future.

The contribution in chapter 3 by Ira Robinson of the Department of Religion at Concordia University is of a different nature. The tumultuous media campaign that preceded the creation of the Bouchard-Taylor Commission in 2007, and the examples that were singled out in the press as indicative of abuse on the part of a few religious communities, often centred on the behaviour of the Hasidic communities of Outremont. The reasons for this are easy to understand: while Sikhs, Muslims, and Buddhists often congregate in temples situated in the far suburbs of Montreal, many of the Hasidim live in plain sight of the more affluent francophone intelligentsia living on the north slopes of Mount Royal in the Montréal borough of Outremont. Daily encounters on the streets and the complex series of demands on the part of the Hassidim at the municipal level, notably for the building of synagogues, community centres, and schools, have heightened the sense in the francophone press that ultra-orthodox Jews ultimately personify a staunch resistance to laïcité and accommodement raisonnable. It is not unusual in these circumstances that pictures of Hasidim find their way into the printed media as coded examples of cultural deviance and religious irrationality. Ira Robinson points out in chapter 3 that this has put a great deal of pressure on the organized structures within the Jewish community to present convincing briefs to the Commission, and to offer an answer to the malaise expressed within some francophone circles. By and large, the Canadian Jewish Congress, Québec region; the Jewish General Hospital; and B'nai Brith Canada, although less so in the latter case, sought to reduce the heat of the debate and correct unfounded impressions, notably regarding the cost of kosher food. More likely, argues Robinson, the uneasiness that perpetuates itself in the relationship between members of the Jewish community and the linguistic majority of Québec, be it through the recent debate around reasonable accommodation or through media stereotyping, is probably the result of a broader historical misunderstanding that was never resolved to the satisfaction of either party. According to this author, much remains to be done to foster a constructive dialogue between the two groups that never quite came to terms with each other in the recent past.

The briefs presented to the Commission by ordinary citizens are the subject of a study by Concordia University professor Bina Toledo Freiwald (chapter 4) entitled, 'Qui est nous? Some Answers from the Bouchard-Taylor Commission's Archive.' Through a meticulous analysis of the style of writing and the content, these documents reveal how difficult it is for many Québécois to envision a form of civic nationality open to all influences and identities at a time when francophones are still reeling from the changes that have rocked their culture since the Quiet Revolution. In other words, how can the French-speaking majority welcome others when it is uncertain about its own future and what its parameters have become under pressure from mass culture, globalization, and the abandonment of traditional modes of life? According to the author, underlying the tensions experienced in 2006–7 around the accommodement raisonnable is a collision between the values of universalism, to which most cultures aspire and which citizens generally support, and the urge to preserve the originality of a Québécois francophone narrative rooted in peoplehood. Is it conceivable, asks Toledo Freiwald, that such an exercise in democracy, conducted in other parts of Canada and under the guise of multiculturalism, would have produced different results and revealed a more rooted sense of common citizenship? Is universalism in the sphere of human rights and in the construction of a just civic society compatible with particularistic identities, especially when the emotional charge and affective pull of nationalism looms so large in Québec society? The greatest challenge of the Bouchard-Taylor exercise was precisely the reconciling of these two powerful underlying forces under a common interculturalist policy, a task which will require, if ever fully achieved, several more years to come to fruition.

Ultimately there are no clear and definite answers to all these questions. By shifting the emphasis of the Commission on the protection of Québec's francophone identity and by proposing a rather moderate form of 'laïcité,' the two co-chairs were probably trying to attain a broader consensus, which is still lacking around those issues. That they did not have to take into consideration a broader federal and pan-Canadian perspective also played a role in the ultimate wording of the report, which addressed itself exclusively to the Québec provincial area of jurisdiction. This, of course, leaves the exercise open to many interpretations, often very different in tone and conclusion, such as those defended by various academics in this book. Perhaps one should rejoice in such a diversity of opinion, as much as one should celebrate cultural and religious pluralism. As for myself, I remain convinced that this country is too vast, too complex, and too multiple to entertain only one ideology pertaining to heterogeneity. If diversity is an asset, and it certainly is, then multiculturalism can coexist side by side with interculturalism, not to mention other options in the matter such as those defended by Aboriginal communities. After all, it is not uncommon for First Nations to seriously criticize or reject prevailing notions of citizenship in Canada on the basis of its colonial character and oppressive quality.

Meanwhile, Bouchard and Taylor proposed a long series of recommendations, some 30 in all, which included a search for a better definition of laïcité and interculturalism within the Québec context. The priority recommendations of the Commission were (1) to call for a definition of new policies and programs pertaining to interculturalism, notably through legislation and a white paper on secularism; (2) to intensify the recognition of immigrants' skills and diplomas, francization programs, the regionalization of immigration, and the need for more coordination between departments; (3) to demand a broader training of government agents, especially in the public schools, with respect to intercultural practices; (4) to disseminate and promote knowledge of interculturalism in all institutions within civil society; and (5) to intensify the fight against inequality and discrimination. Special attention was also given in the report to the situation of women in the immigrant milieus, and to the fundamental question of the equality of sexes. In fact, the gender issue became so prevalent in the round of consultations carried by the Commission that one of the charges frequently levelled against certain minorities was their supposedly unjust treatment of women. Many feminists even went so far as to equate tolerance of religious diversity with an abandonment of the basic rights of women as embodied in the Québec charter of rights.

Meanwhile, it quickly became evident that the apprehended crisis in Québec society provoked by les accommodements raisonnables, swelled by politicians and media alike, had simply not really taken place. Brief after brief from social and public health organizations reached the Commission stressing the artificial character of the debate supported by

Bouchard and Taylor. They claimed that ways and means to accommodate the tide of immigration had long been reached in Montreal. Cultural diversity and religious pluralism in certain neighbourhoods of Québec's largest city had become commonplace, and examples of adjustment and adaptation simply more widespread than instances of conflict or confrontation. In the last analysis, it finally appeared that much of the impetus to create the Commission had been purely opportunistic, and discussions around the issue were mostly of an ideological nature. Rather than take the matter into his own hands politically, and reaffirm the principles at the basis for the current policies regarding diversity and immigrant integration, Premier Charest preferred to win time and submit the question to an external body. This conclusion became even more evident on 22 May 2008, when the premier immediately rejected one of the recommendations made the very same day by Bouchard and Taylor, to relocate the crucifix above the chair of the president of the National Assembly, Québec's provincial parliament.

In the weeks that followed, Charest did little to implement the suggestions made by the co-chairs, whether in the broader sense or by supporting minor changes in the already existing structures of government, leaving the Commission to fend off criticism alone. Soon Charest was on the campaign trail, and on 8 December 2008, he was re-elected premier of Québec for the third consecutive term, dealing at the same time a deathly blow to the Action démocratique du Québec and its anti-accommodationist leader Mario Dumont. With the global economic slowdown experienced since the end of 2008, and the pressing problems of unemployment and budget deficits, there is little likelihood that the debate on cultural diversity will resurface with such urgency in the near future.

The Bouchard-Taylor report was generally well received by the organizations that represent Montreal's cultural communities, notably Muslims, Jews, and other religious minorities. Most of the recommendations made by the co-chairs proposed reinforcing the measures already in place to integrate the immigrants and fight against all forms of discrimination, and thus were not found lacking in content and scope. As support for interculturalism is almost universal in Québec, calls to better define and apply the concept were also well received. Most critics, and some of them bitterly, tended to focus on laïcité and women's rights. Several workers' unions found the proposals to be too soft, and likely to perpetuate a situation where religious minorities use each item of human rights legislation available to advance their agenda, notably vis-à-vis a possibly differential treatment of women. On the other hand, the Canadian Jewish Congress denounced the limitations placed by the Commission on state officials and judges wearing headgear and other outward signs of faith. Clearly these two issues remain the most sensitive ones in Québec society today, and are the ones most likely to create social tensions in the future no matter how small and trivial the matter at hand. On this point, the co-chairs could not arrive at a generally acceptable solution, and, in a way, disappointed almost every lobby group by seeking an elusive middle ground. The Commission was also attacked viciously by some nationalist groups who are generally staunch opponents of multiculturalism, including former Péquiste premiers Jacques Parizeau and Bernard Landry, on the grounds that Bouchard and Taylor proposed little to promote the inclusion of recent immigrants into French-speaking milieus and tended to blame the French majority for its lack of tolerance. This was a personal blow to Gérard Bouchard, whose brother was elected premier of Québec in 1996 as head of the Parti Québécois while he himself was a prominent mouthpiece of the sovereignist movement. Such reactions do indicate nonetheless how much of the debate on accommodement raisonnable hinges ultimately in the minds of many citizens on the perpetuation of a Québécois identity. Clearly, in certain circles, there can be little tolerance of cultural and religious diversity unless strong measures are in place to guarantee the future of the French language in the Montreal region.

There is no doubt in my mind that the Bouchard-Taylor Commission was a watershed in the debate on cultural diversity in Québec, if only because it gave citizens from all walks of life and on a wide regional base the occasion to express themselves on a theme crucial to the future of their society. This in a sense was a major innovation presented by the Commission, even though it led at times to racist and xenophobic pronouncements, which, sadly, the co-chairs did not always see fit to contradict on the spot. In many ways, this was both the crowning achievement and the undoing of the Commission, as neither Bouchard nor Taylor had the political experience or the personal credentials to redirect the strong flow of ideas that emerged pell-mell out of the consultations. One could also argue that this public outpouring of emotion, especially around such an abstract notion as accommodement raisonnable, is in many ways a feature of Québec's political culture. It remains doubtful that such a climate of participation could have developed in other parts of Canada in quite the same fashion. Bouchard and Taylor manoeuvred in the midst of a public mood that was reminiscent, to a degree, of the 1995 referendum and the fundamental question that it posed. This approach by the Commission tended to overdramatize the debate in the eyes of outsiders, and perhaps produced an overblown picture of the tensions existing within Québec's society around issues of cultural and religious tolerance. For all its failings and limitations, not the least of which is its inability to convince the government to act more boldly in the short term, the Bouchard-Taylor Commission will leave a lasting legacy as a serious attempt to mobilize all segments of the population and come to some form of understanding as to the breadth of the debate. The report itself, despite being paternalistic in tone and perhaps somewhat too didactic, will no doubt be consulted in the future as an important milestone. It is also likely to leave its mark on all public policies directed to diversity in anglophone Canada, in francophone Europe, and in the rest of the world. Our final chapter and conclusion takes up the significant long-term and globalized impact of the Bouchard-Taylor Report on the issue of diversity, which is an ever-present feature of all societies in the modern, globalized world.

1 Reasonable Accommodation in the Canadian Legal Context: A Mechanism for Managing Diversity or a Source of Tension?

PIERRE ANCTIL

Many historical, legal, and cultural factors have contributed to the evolution of the Canadian identity throughout the twentieth century, not the least of which was the transition from the status of British colony to that of sovereign state within the British Commonwealth and the international community of nations. At first Canada was seen by the main English elite as simply an appendage of the Empire on the North American continent and thus dependent on London. Gradually, however, it acquired its own distinct personality thanks to events that had a significant impact on British imperialism, for example, the Boer revolt of 1899–1902 and the two world wars. At the time of the signing of the British North America Act, the statute enacted by the London Parliament, which was to give birth in 1867 to the Dominion of Canada, the prevailing sentiment in English Canada was that the country had to conform in every way to the economic and imperial demands of the motherland. This meant rushing to the aid of Great Britain when it was the object of serious military threats or needed the help of its colonies in the international arena, for example, sending military contingents or promoting the purchase of British industrial products. In fact, until the Second World War, many Canadians of British origin did not see a great difference in interests between Great Britain and their own country, to the point where creating a systematic policy of Canadian national autonomy within the Empire seemed unnecessary to them. This dominant viewpoint was reinforced for a long time by the fear that the neighbouring American republic would try to forcibly acquire all or part of the vast Canadian territory in the context of its own expansionism, notably right after the Civil War of 1861–5 when the government in Washington had at its disposal large, well-trained armies.

Eventually, many elements radically modified this vision of a Canada developing under the wing of British imperialism and enjoying the privileged status of 'White Dominion' in the midst of a political reality marked by pronounced racial stratification among the colonies. Subjected to the will of London after 1763, the inhabitants of the defunct French establishment in North America demanded and received, beginning with the Québec Act of 1774, several decisive political and constitutional advantages, such as retaining the French civil law, the possibility as Catholics to hold elective or governmental posts, and the right to use French as a public and official language. Settled on the continent since the beginning of the seventeenth century and possessing a unique culture as North Americans, the francophones in Canada formed a deeply rooted, distinct community, essentially left intact by the British conquest. For a long time the French Canadians were more numerous demographically than their English counterparts, and they later constituted a large majority in the St Lawrence Valley.

Thus, after the federal accord of 1867, they were generally the first to demand the recognition of a Canadian identity separate from the narrow political and cultural framework in which London hoped to keep its Canadian colony. This is how, first in an embryonic way at the beginning of the nineteenth century, and then more and more insistently, the idea arose that the newly born Canadian state was the outcome of an honourable compromise between two founding nations and was home to a population originating from two great European cultures. For the French Canadians, the reality of a country independent from Great Britain's colonial ambitions seemed self-evident, especially in the context of a Canadianization imposed by the geography of the continent and its substantial distance from Europe.

The insistence of French Canadians on releasing their country from the clutches of British imperialism was also expressed at the beginning of the twentieth century, in tandem with the rise of nationalist movements in several of London's colonies, such as Ireland, Scotland, India, Australia, and South Africa. In this sense Canada followed a trajectory quite common within the Empire, and which was often led by linguistic minorities or populations whose origins were more or less far removed from that of the English Protestant elites. Nevertheless, this chipping away in favour of a much more Canadian nationalism took almost a century to reach its goal, from the establishment of a responsible government around 1840 until the end of the Second World War; such was the extent of the English Canadians' attachment to their motherland

and the advantages that came with British citizenship modelled on the Empire. Throughout this long process, whose consequences were not really felt until the 1960s and 1970s, other significant historical events occurred that would exert a decisive influence on the evolution of Canadian identity. Foremost was the great wave of immigration of 1905–14, and, after 1930, the weighty impact of the American republic on Canada's economic development. By the beginning of the twentieth century, Canadians had come to accept, often reluctantly, that their country was composed of two European populations, quite close in origin but prevented from merging together by colonial and political rivalries.

In 1867, when the country was founded under the aegis of Great Britain, a series of administrative and legal mechanisms were put in place that guaranteed the use of separate educational institutions for both Catholics and Protestants. This meant that francophones and anglophones rarely interacted with each other in the spheres of education and philanthropy, or in the domains either closely or remotely related to religious life. Gradually, especially in Montreal, Canada established itself around two parallel linguistic communities whose allegiances and interests were very different, both politically and socio-economically. This tendency was reinforced by the evolution of the Canadian federation, where regional identities were fostered thanks to the existence of provinces, each having an autonomous parliament and some budgetary room to manoeuvre, as well as exclusive powers. One province in particular, Québec, became the rallying point for French Catholics, whereas Ontario came to represent the Anglo-Protestant majority in the country. This national duality became so entrenched in Canadian institutions, and in life generally, that it was reflected even in the nomination of judges to the Supreme Court, in the linguistic alternation of the country's prime ministers, and in the existence of two cultural and intellectual elites that rarely communicated with each other.

The country was, however, severely underpopulated at the time of its founding in 1867. Further, its population was almost completely concentrated in the St Lawrence Valley and on the northern shores of the Great Lakes, which made it easy prey for American expansionism. Faced with this situation, Prime Minister John A. Macdonald, elected in 1867, decided to put in place a national policy aimed at correcting the geographical and political disadvantages with which Canada was afflicted since its birth. These included the absence of large-scale railway transport, an underdeveloped interior economic market, and vast territories in the west still under the direct tutelage of the British Crown.

The Canadian transcontinental railway line did not come into existence until the 1880s, and the Great Plains were not accessible until several years after that. It was therefore incumbent upon Macdonald's successor as head of state, Sir Wilfred Laurier, to establish a comprehensive plan to bring into Canada a foreign workforce drawn from the vast populations of eastern and southern Europe. While only five million people lived in Canada in 1901, administrative and consular measures were put in place to receive as of that date tens of thousands, if not hundreds of thousands, of new people every year.

Between 1905 and 1914, until the beginning of the First World War, close to two million immigrants found their way to Canada, mostly nationals from the Russian Empire, the Central Powers, the Balkans, Greece, and Italy. This influx of people was supposed to settle in the vast territories west of Ontario, particularly the provinces of Saskatchewan and Alberta, created in 1905. However, it was not long before these new arrivals gravitated to the important Canadian cities of that time, Montreal and Toronto, where large enclaves were formed, populated by recently arrived individuals who were not fluent in either of the two official languages. Most importantly, the arrival of large contingents of people of Russian, Ukrainian, Polish, German, Italian, and Jewish descent, and their subsequent dispersal throughout Canada, deeply transformed the ethnic composition of the principal regions and introduced a linguistic and cultural diversification that until then had been absent.

At the end of the nineteenth century, Canada saw itself more or less accurately as the heir of British and French colonial efforts in North America. It was then that a new historical conjuncture brought to its coasts substantial numbers of people with very different religious and cultural traditions, who soon began to demand the right to full participation in the political institutions of the country. It is true that Canadians, who were not above racial discrimination and prejudice of all kinds, often resorted, during the twentieth century, to less than glorious subterfuges to keep certain communities from gaining power, or to exclude them completely from the political and socio-economic arena, as seen in various historical episodes dealing with the arrival of Japanese and Chinese nationals on the Pacific coast, as well as the problems experienced by Jews, Blacks, and Asians in major Canadian cities.

In fact, not until 1967 was a system introduced in Canada that selected immigrants based on their skills and aptitudes, and did not, at least outwardly, take into account the national origin, colour, or religious beliefs of those aspiring to become Canadian citizens. The immigration policies of the Canadian state, practiced over a long period, profoundly changed the balance of power between the two founding communities of the country and the new arrivals of increasingly diverse origins. Gradually, and especially after the 1980s, the percentage of foreign-born people in large Canadian urban centres began to climb, as did the percentage of individuals whose origin was other than French or English, so much so that immigrants today account for nearly 20 per cent of the country's population, originating mainly from Asia, Africa, Latin America, and Eastern Europe.

The Trudeau Years

The above, roughly sketched historical events had a strong influence on the post-war development of an official ideology aimed at establishing for the first time the specific parameters of a Canadian citizenry and identity. The 1960s, 1970s, and 1980s were particularly productive in this regard, as three fundamental orientations were set forth thanks to the mandate of Pierre Trudeau at the helm of the federal government. These were: the Official Languages Act of 1969, the declaration of a policy on multiculturalism in 1971, and the introduction in 1982 of the Charter of Rights and Freedoms following the repatriation of the Constitution. In the first case, it was a matter of giving the French language equal status to that of English in domains under federal jurisdiction, and a more effective support for French and English minorities, notably through the creation of the Office of the Commissioner of Official Languages. This act was in fact meant to be a response to the Royal Commission on Bilingualism and Biculturalism (which had held discussions several years earlier amidst rather intense controversy), as well as to the political tensions emanating from a full-blown cultural upheaval in Québec society.

Only two years after the proclamation of the Official Languages Act in 1971, Prime Minister Trudeau declared that if Canada henceforth had two official languages, no specific culture could be considered the primary reflection of the life of the country. As for recently arrived immigrants, they were invited to honour and publicly celebrate their heritage just as much as the two founding communities. Thus, whereas Canadians could communicate with the federal government as much in French as in English, that did not oblige them to conform to the cultural values of French or English Canada, nor to adopt the point of view of the majority, essentially of European origin.

The Official Languages Act and the policy on multiculturalism awarded certain privileges to individuals on the basis of recognized collective identities, notably by relying on linguistic, cultural, and religious heritages specific to the Canadian historical framework. On the other hand, the Canadian Charter of Rights and Freedoms of 1982 primarily upheld the supremacy of individual rights with respect to the powers of the state. Promulgated thanks to the Canadianization of the constitution of 1867, the Charter broke with British legal tradition, which had been the norm in the country until then, and introduced for the first time in Canadian political history the more American notion of a supreme law that formally regulates relations between the individual and the state. In the years that followed, the Canadian government completely changed its discourse on Canadian identity and sought to calibrate its interventions by repeatedly referring to the founding texts on the official languages, on multiculturalism, and those concerning the fundamental rights and freedoms proclaimed in the Charter.

Already one of the most decentralized federations on the planet, notably in the area of relations between the provinces and the central government, Canada formalized the idea that there were many different and sometimes contradictory ways to be a Canadian. It affirmed that there was no such thing as an official culture in the country, and reiterated that it was possible to legislate on the linguistic front without offending the cultural and religious values of individuals. The government was actually challenged in this context by the claims of the Aboriginal peoples, who wanted to push the country even further in the direction of decentralization by recalling that the First Nations had already existed as fully autonomous communities for a long time before the emergence of the Canadian state. Indeed, no sooner had Canadian citizenship been redefined by a new constitutional text than it was attacked by certain First Nations people who went as far as to claim the right to ignore or reject what they saw as the primarily Eurocentric principles of the 1982 Charter.

The deconstruction of the official Canadian identity, the one being promoted by the federal government both at home and abroad, continued with the proclamation, in 1988, of a law on multiculturalism. At first multiculturalism had been perceived during the 1970s and 1980s as a positive support for the folkloristic traditions of recent immigrants originating mainly from a variety of Asian, African, and South American countries. It was not long, however, before multiculturalism adopted the language of the struggle against racial discrimination and ethnocentric prejudice. The more cultural and religious diversity grew in Canada, largely due to an aggressive immigration policy, the more it became urgent to contain within reasonable limits the hostile opinions regarding the growing presence of people and communities of non-European origin within the Canadian population.

The Canadian state, therefore, made a point of reminding everyone after 1988 that new citizens and their descendants remained free to adhere or not to adhere to the cultural values of the Canadian population already in place, both French and English, and that assimilationism was not part of the strategies chosen to deal with the substantial migratory movement directed towards Canada. 'It is hereby declared to be the policy of the Government of Canada to recognize and promote the understanding that multiculturalism reflects the cultural and racial diversity of Canadian society and acknowledges the freedom of all members of Canadian society to preserve, enhance and share their cultural heritage.'[1] Furthermore, the government in Ottawa was ready to recognize that those groups speaking non-official languages were free, if they so desired, to build community infrastructures aimed at preserving their cultural and religious traditions in their new country, a principle which is reflected in the 1988 Multiculturalism Act in the following way: 'To recognize the existence of communities whose members share a common origin and their historic contribution to Canadian society, and enhance their development.'[2] In many cases this political support went as far as giving financial assistance for specific projects in the framework of programs under the authority of the Secretary of State or the Ministry of Multiculturalism.

Multiculturalism was generally very well accepted by Canadians, except in the one province with a francophone majority, where resistance developed, not around the concept of cultural and religious diversity, but rather with respect to the indifference of this federal policy regarding the linguistic question. Indeed, to francophones, multiculturalism seemed language-blind and had been designed as a completely separate responsibility within the federal government dating from the Official Languages Act of 1969. In Québec, the integration of new arrivals into the French language, that is, into the French demographic majority, seemed more urgent as well as more difficult to effectuate. While immigrants in Vancouver, Calgary, and Toronto found it normal and acceptable to learn English in order to succeed at integrating economically into Canadian society, it was quite different in Montreal where French seemed a lot less attractive and less likely to be adopted as a priority by newcomers.

To counter this imbalance caused by the less prestigious status of the French language as a vehicle of integration into the Canadian, or rather North American, landscape, the Québec government, at the end of the 1970s, hastened to set forth its own version of multiculturalism. It was known as 'interculturalism,' taking the basic principles of the federal ideology and adding a linguistic component designed to guarantee that immigrants would integrate into the Québec French-speaking majority. Being vulnerable as an official language minority within the Canadian federation, the Québec francophones thus reaffirmed their commitment to the values of pluralism and diversity while also taking measures to prevent the worsening, through the anglicization of immigrants, of the existing historical linguistic imbalance within Canada. Namely, with this step, francophone Québecers were able to join the multicultural movement, renamed interculturalism in their distinct society: 'Québec designates its policy as "interculturalism." It is mainly concerned with the acceptance of and communication and interaction between culturally diverse groups, without, however, implying any intrinsic equality among them. Diversity is tolerated and encouraged, but only within a framework that establishes the unquestioned supremacy of French in the language and culture of Québec.'[3]

As it turned out, however, the linguistic law of 1969 and the declaration on multiculturalism of 1971, including the constitutionalization of the principle of cultural diversity in 1982, held no more than symbolic value in the Canadian political arena. On the one hand, individuals have very little direct contact with the federal bureaucracy; on the other, the sums of money set aside for these issues on an annual basis are quite modest. Moreover, the main actors on the cultural and linguistic stage in Canada are still the provincial governments; in many cases the policies and programs established by the provincial capitals have contradicted the principles of the federal official languages law of 1969. In the end, only New Brunswick applied the principle of bilingualism in its integral form as proposed by Ottawa. In most cases, the anglophone provinces did not propose any significant measures aimed at protecting their francophone minorities, except in the area of education, and even that was under the constraint of Article 23 of the Constitution Act of 1982.

As for multiculturalism, it is easy to see that this is essentially an abstract form of discussion used by the government to better define the notion of Canadian citizenship. Combating racism, opening to diversity, welcoming immigrants, and promoting full democratic participation constitute the principal aspects of the law of 1988, with a sometimes more symbolic than tangible support to the cultural affirmation of communities other than the francophones or anglophones. As in the case of the official languages, the provinces and municipalities have generally abstained from effectively intervening in the sphere of multiculturalism, or to relay the federal message in this regard.

It was a very different scenario with the Charter of Rights and Freedoms. As soon as it was declared in 1982, it became the object of an intense societal debate, not only because the Canadian constitution was repatriated in a climate of acrimonious political strife between the provinces and the federal government, but also because it represented to many observers an attempt to impose foreign legal notions on the British tradition, which had prevailed throughout the history of the country until this time. The supreme law of Canada was conceived after the two official languages had been proclaimed, after the ancestral rights of the First Nations had been declared irrevocable, and after the minorities of immigrant origin had been formally recognized within the framework of multiculturalism.

In this context, the application of a charter that upholds above all else the fundamental rights of the individual was bound to come up against the affirmation of the collective values of certain vulnerable populations, either linguistically, culturally, or communally. As we will soon see, people belonging to Canadian minority nations and groups were quick to understand that the Charter cleared the way for bringing a new kind of collective claim before the human rights tribunals, as long as it was presented as an act of discrimination, not against a particular community, but rather against an individual identified as a member of a specific minority group. In the beginning, the Charter based itself on the premise that the individual had the right to be protected, within reasonable limits, from abuse and excesses committed by the government in its governing of the country. It was also possible to obtain redress in cases where certain social behaviour or mechanisms in the private sector violated fundamental individual rights as defined in Article 2; that is, essentially, freedom of conscience, religion, belief, and opinion, as well as the freedom of association and peaceful assembly.

Furthermore, the Charter protects individuals who choose to adopt multiple and sometimes contradictory identities that do not respect the generally accepted social or cultural norms, or who uphold interpretations that are novel and innovative compared to criteria historically recognized in Canada, including those dealing with religion, spiritual beliefs, or external signs of one's faith. The fundamental law would even come to the defence of people who refused to accept as valid and justified the perspective put forth by the new Canadian legal culture. One example could be a case where people belonging to First Nations' traditionalist movements declare themselves to be religious fundamentalists or reject the relevance of Western notions of freedom and justice.[4] Then there could be those who prefer to adopt a resolutely anarchist perspective, or who favour communitarianism, or who consider the Canadian state to be an illegitimate expression of British imperialism.

Moreover, although the 1982 Charter makes no direct reference to the presumed secularism of the Canadian state, or to the obligation of its representatives and public servants to maintain, in their functions, absolute neutrality with respect to the expression of religious beliefs, recent court cases have made it abundantly clear that the Canadian government was committed to benevolent neutrality in the face of this phenomenon, and that it could not favour one religious tradition to the detriment of another. Proclaimed more than 25 years ago, the Charter created a new movement in the evolution of Canadian law of which we are only now beginning to assess the long-term consequences.

Many studies and analyses have demonstrated that the principle, affirmed in the Charter, of strict equality of individuals before the law, conceived as a fundamental right and as legal protection against discrimination, has not really improved the situation of people belonging to certain minority nations or communities who are victims of systematic discrimination within society in general or in specific work environments. Despite unceasing government campaigns and the repeated affirmation of the equality of all before the law, racism, prejudice, and xenophobia persist in Canada. Thus, differences in treatment according to colour, national origin, and language are still very present in certain sectors of the economy and at certain levels of society. Writers and academics, notably those who are themselves recent immigrants, such as Neil Bissoondath (1994) in a widely discussed essay, have pointed out that the federal ideology of multiculturalism has sometimes tended to confine individuals belonging to visible minorities inside specific parameters of identity which did not encourage, among other things, their full integration into the political and social life of Canada. By thus creating categories of individuals to whom specific programs are offered, even while championing a positive attitude towards differences, the Canadian government was sometimes inadvertently guilty of perpetuating, under a different guise, divisions already existing in the country, or of drawing attention to issues of specific identity that the individuals concerned preferred to overcome in another way. We can thus see that in many instances the charter of fundamental rights and the federal ideology of multiculturalism have managed to limit the expression of the most flagrant forms of racism and discrimination without really attacking the root of the problem or putting an end to the social mechanisms that create the inequalities.

One of the possible solutions to this dilemma emerged as a typically Canadian legal concept known as 'reasonable accommodation.' This states that in obvious cases of discrimination, in the case of a particular plaintiff, the courts may agree to an adjustment of a universally applicable legal regulation. This option thus prevents, in certain specific cases, a tribunal's just and equitable ruling – arrived at with respect to a general situation – from perpetuating or reproducing injustices when applied to an individual belonging to a national minority, an Aboriginal community, or any other group recognized as being the target of unacceptable forms of prejudice. It is also possible to use reasonable accommodation to deal with the situation of people identified in the Charter as being vulnerable to certain violations of their fundamental rights, such as the handicapped, pregnant women, people with a minority sexual orientation, or those who publicly affirm their religious beliefs.

From many points of view, this new concept appears to be a unique contribution to the jurisprudence associated with handling diversity in a context where Canada also recognizes the existence of collective rights in the form of two official languages, self-governance of First Nations' peoples, and the promotion of cultural and religious plurality. Yet it is a mechanism of legal arbitration that has not been used very often, only 73 times during the last 22 years, although the rate of use has accelerated during the last 10 years.[5] It is also important to note that the courts (mainly the superior ones rather than the lower courts) have resorted to reasonable accommodation to settle disputes related to discrimination of one sort or another.

It would be worthwhile, as part of this chapter, to examine many of the judgments dealing with reasonable accommodation to better elucidate this Canadian legal concept. Due to lack of space, we will look at three specific examples that clearly illustrate its parameters and that had a significant impact on the related jurisprudence and on the public in general. They are, in chronological order, the wearing of a Sikh turban by a member of the Royal Canadian Mounted Police while carrying out his official duties (1995); the erection of a *sukkah* (a temporary hut in which a family eats its meals during Sukkot, the week-long Jewish Feast of Tabernacles) on a private balcony by the owners of a condominium, more precisely at the Sanctuaire du Mont Royal luxury condominium complex in Montreal (2004); and, lastly, the wearing of a kirpan in class by a student at a high school in LaSalle in suburban Montreal (2006). In each case, the judges asked that an exception be made to the general regulations governing the functioning of a specific public or private organization; that is, those of the Canadian federal police, the contract outlining the rights and obligations of condominium owners, and those of a school commission. This would allow individuals adhering to a particular religious belief to act according to the dictates of their faith. In each instance the judges defended the point of view that to proceed otherwise would deny these people their inalienable right to exercise their freedom of religious expression. In the eyes of the courts, to apply a general regulation in the cases of these plaintiffs would have opened the door to a form of discrimination considered unacceptable according to the Charter, especially since the above-mentioned federal police officer, condominium owner, and high-school student belong to recognized religious minorities that are liable to be targets of prejudice viewed as unacceptable in the context of Canadian democracy.

The interpretation of the Charter of Rights and Freedoms used during the last few years with respect to certain plaintiffs reflecting the national, cultural, and religious diversity of Canada, has had the paradoxical effect of reinforcing the multicultural ideology of the country as well as a whole set of collective values. While this fundamental Canadian law was enacted primarily to protect the individual against the arbitrariness of the state, we are beginning to see now that it can also indirectly support claims of a communal nature or those relating to minority identities. This is clearly a turnaround not foreseen in the short term at the time of the declaration on multiculturalism of 1971, nor the law of 1988 on the same theme, both of which were drawn up in very general terms with little in the way of restraint for public administrations or private enterprises. The movement in this direction was soon perceived by certain religious or cultural minorities recently settled in Canada, and they quickly developed legal strategies for the purpose of demanding special applications and reasonable accommodations from the justice courts of this country. These strategies, often sophisticated in their objective comprehension of the Charter, frequently come from groups or communities who at first refuse to integrate into the prevailing political liberalism or to abandon their traditional religious practices, but understand very well the benefits to be garnered from having recourse to Canadian fundamental rights. In one sense, we find in these strategies one more indication that Canada is succeeding in inculcating in all its inhabitants, even those who defend a communitarian and traditional approach to life and society, the idea that there is a place for negotiation and dialogue within the public arena to which all can have recourse in case of apparent conflict or discord.

The Bouchard-Taylor Commission

Reasonable accommodation must therefore be considered, first and foremost, as a legal tool that allows for the just and equitable treatment before Canadian law, of people belonging to a minority experiencing discrimination. It can in fact happen that a general judgment meant to respect fundamental rights in a reasonable way actually produces negative and restrictive effects when applied to individuals already liable, for historical or other reasons, to be treated unjustly in the labour market or in public life in general. Thus, it frequently happens in Canada, especially in the large cities with their rich linguistic, cultural, and religious diversity, that negotiations and adjustments are necessary to enable the full participation of individuals belonging to communities that adhere to particular values and beliefs. Sometimes these exchanges occur at the private level between individuals from differing backgrounds, and sometimes they involve government agencies, public enterprises, or municipalities.

In fact, in the majority of cases, differences of opinion or interpretation among adherents of different cultural or religious traditions are resolved amicably without intervention of the state or the courts; they do not require the mediation of a superior authority. Indeed, holding a trial where reasonable accommodation in its legal form is invoked, and therefore made binding by order of the court, has been more the exception than the rule. During the last few years, several highly publicized cases have nevertheless drawn the attention of the public to the question of reasonable accommodation, including the above-mentioned three rulings. These have led to the erroneous belief that certain cultural and religious minorities were receiving preferential treatment in Canada when they demanded adjustments to practices currently enforced in society. While the ideology of multiculturalism and the declaration on Canadian citizenship had until that point set forth only very broad lines of conduct concerning possible areas of conflict around diversity within Canadian society, at the beginning of the twenty-first century everything seems to indicate that having recourse to the Charter of Rights and Freedoms opens up much more promising avenues for minorities.

These perceptions were particularly vivid when the debates focused on religious issues affecting the presumed neutrality of the public space or when they put the spotlight on groups living in a densely concentrated way in certain residential areas. Issues of equal treatment for people of both genders, present in many of these cases, also greatly contributed to raising the temperature of the discussions around these questions. In Montreal, and other places where the presence in certain neighbourhoods of Hasidic, Muslim, or Sikh minorities is quite visible, the media have displayed, sometimes on the front page, a whole series of demands regarding the intermingling in certain institutions or in the public space of people of diverse origins. Among the most well-known are the problems between the Hasidic Satmar community and a community/ sports centre subsidized by the municipality;[6] the unregulated setting up of synagogues in private residences; the requests for special time slots reserved for women only at municipal pools; the availability of kosher or hallal food in hospitals and health care centres; the honouring of religious calendars belonging to Judaism, Islam, or other religious traditions including Christian fundamentalists; and, last but not least, the desire of users to have access to professionals and public servants of the same gender as themselves. Nonetheless, contrary to the three incidents mentioned earlier (the kirpan in the school, the headgear used by RCMP officers, and the sukkah erected in a condominium), none of these cases were brought before a court of justice nor were they dealt with by means of reasonable accommodation in the legal sense. Quite simply, the various parties on either side of the disputes in question preferred to rely on their own judgment and the goodwill of all concerned.

These issues, on the part of the public and many journalists, have nevertheless continued during the last few years, notably in Québec where an escalation in the media as well as in the political arena finally led to the creation, in February 2007, of an official body named the Consultation Commission on Accommodation Practices Related to Cultural Differences. There is no reason to believe that cultural diversity is less well accepted in Québec than in the rest of Canada, or that racism and xenophobia are more intensely present. One cannot deny, however, that the immigration issue in Montreal is distinctly different, notably with respect to language. There is a greater sensitivity in Québec than in the other largely anglophone provinces when it comes to the place of religion in the public space. We have seen that Canadian multiculturalism as an ideology of the Canadian state does not take into account the language factor, and language is at the centre of the 1969 federal law on official languages. Multiculturalism welcomes cultural pluralism as a phenomenon separate from any other reality. In Québec, this approach is often decried by the nationalist movements as potentially leading to the marginalization of the francophone reality, particularly in Montreal where the adoption of English by new immigrants could sound the death knell in the long run for the desired predominance of French in the public arena.

French Canadian culture, before the Quiet Revolution of the 1960s, was also characterized by a strong religious presence in political life, due mainly to the adherence of the vast majority of French-speaking people to the Catholic faith. The will of the Church to manage large sections of the institutional structure of French Canada was completely rejected at the time of Québec's modernization, to the point where this rejection may explain in part why the demands of religious minorities are often less well treated in this context than in English Canada. We must also consider the fact that political debates often take on a more intense and insistent tone in francophone Québec, a society where people do not hesitate to bring difficult questions to the fore and engage in spirited discussion.

The Consultation Commission on Accommodation Practices Related to Cultural Differences was entrusted to two renowned academics, Gérard Bouchard and Charles Taylor, who each represent one aspect of Québec public life. The first is a francophone belonging to the sovereignist movement, while the second espouses the historical values of the Canadian state. Supported by a team of researchers, they were given the mandate by the Québec government to take stock of the practices of adjustment to cultural and religious diversity being carried out in Québec, those that go beyond the strictly legal notion known as reasonable accommodation. They were also given the responsibility of conducting an extensive consultation on this subject in all the regions, and 'to formulate recommendations to the government to ensure that accommodation practices conform to the values of Québec society as a pluralist, democratic, egalitarian society.'[7] The Commission was required, on the one hand, to confine its deliberations to all forms of arrangements 'allowed by managers in public or private institutions in respect of students, patients, customers, employees and so on,'[8] and, on the other hand, to examine in a broader sense the intercultural integration model established in Québec 30 years ago, as opposed to the Canadian government, which, during the same period, had favoured a notion of multiculturalism without including the idea of secularism. Over the course of this exercise, which lasted about 10 months in total, the Commission held sessions in 22 regions, received more than 900 briefs coming from individuals and groups, and heard testimony given by more than 240 people during 31 days of public hearings.

The conclusions and recommendations of the Bouchard-Taylor Commission were made public in Montreal on 22 May 2008 amidst intense media hype and after many months of anticipation. The elected members of the Québec National Assembly, as well as the representatives of various interest groups, such as the civil service of Québec and the municipalities, the service providers in the health care and social services system, public sector teachers, unions, and spokespeople for various cultural communities, all eagerly pounced on the document when it was released. At the outset, the two co-presidents declared that the perceived crisis in the handling of cultural diversity in Québec and in the integration of new arrivals, which the creation of the Commission itself seemed to confirm, simply did not exist on the ground:

> After a year of research and consultation, we have come to the conclusion that the foundations of collective life in Québec are not in a critical situation. Our investigation did not reveal to us a striking or sudden increase in the adjustments or accommodation that public institutions allow, nor did we observe that the normal operation of our institutions would have been disrupted by such requests ... We also observed a certain discrepancy between practices in the field, especially in the education and health sectors, and the feeling of discontent that has arisen among Québecers.[9]

In fact, nothing led one to believe that the situation of cultural or religious minorities in Montreal had been radically altered during the months preceding the nomination of Gérard Bouchard and Charles Taylor to head the Commission, nor that the real or perceived deterioration in the francization sector or in the handling of requests from certain communities were having any particular repercussions. Such an acknowledgment greatly contributed to putting the debates of the previous months into perspective and calming things down around a discussion that had been the object of a kind of media hysteria. In fact, these remarks had been anticipated by observers of the Montreal scene and by those who were familiar with the institutions and public service systems most affected by Montreal plurality. Was it really worth it to embark upon such a huge undertaking only to arrive at such reasonable and predictable conclusions? Would it not have been more convincing and more effective for the Charest government itself to act on the diversity dossier several months earlier and to indicate the direction and the means by which it wished to proceed?

Nevertheless, the Commission did make an important contribution to the debate when it declared that an identity-related malaise was gnawing at the francophone majority with regard to cultural and religious pluralism. This observation was meant to bring attention to the ambivalence and uncertainty of the population of French Canadian descent, which seems to want to both keep intact its sphere of linguistic affirmation and historical heritage, and, at the same time, remain open to the great economic and technological developments sweeping the globe. The complexity of the Commission's mandate and the obstacles that continue to hinder the secure preservation of the French reality in Québec, have, in fact, convinced some francophones to oppose any opening to diversity if that diversity is perceived to be threatening and possibly harmful. While this line of thinking is limited to areas on the outskirts of the greater Montreal region and does not seem to have taken hold among a significant percentage of the French-speaking public, it was sufficiently highlighted in the media and by some sensational declarations to create an often pronounced sentiment of unease:

> In a certain segment of the population, this tension targeted the immigrant, who has become a kind of scapegoat. What has just happened in Québec gives the impression of a face-off between two minority groups each asking the other to accommodate it. The members of the ethnocultural majority are afraid of being submerged by minorities who are themselves fragile and worried about their future. The conjunction of these two anxieties is obviously not conducive to fostering integration in the spirit of equality and reciprocity.[10]

There is no doubt that the Commission brought clarity to this issue by affirming that the community on the receiving end, meaning the demographic majority in Québec, has an undeniable responsibility in the establishment of a climate that fosters dialogue between cultures and the full participation of cultural and religious minorities. This does not mean, as some political pundits will say, that the more marginal communities are relieved of any involvement in the evolution of this debate or of the obligation to adapt to the Québécois context, but rather that the segment of the population most likely to lend a positive tone to the question of reasonable accommodation is the francophone majority. This is without doubt the Commission's most courageous and significant affirmation in view of some peremptory statements made in the last few months before the Commission released its report, which tried to saddle the minority communities with all the costs and obligations associated with a more harmonious integration.

In addition to these more general reflections, the Commission also submitted 37 specific recommendations regarding government intervention in the matter of cultural and religious diversity. For the most part, these measures are likely to be unanimously accepted by those groups interested in promoting intercultural dialogue and full minority participation. Among these recommendations we find the promotion of interculturalism by means of legislation, the publication of a policy statement pertaining to diversity and openness to cultural pluralism, the setting up of programs aimed at fostering the accountability of interveners in the various social and government milieus, the intensification of the fight against discrimination and racism, the recognition of immigrants' skills and diplomas, an improved francization of immigrants, and a sensitization of government agents to the wearing of external signs of a person's faith. The Commission also recommended dejudicializing the accommodation practices already in place, improving the expertise of civil servants and other interveners, and sensitizing parents in public and private educational institutions, as well as highlighting the excellence of efforts at harmonization in various workplaces.

Regarding the regionalization of immigration, meaning the opening to diversity in more rural areas of Québec or those on the outskirts of the greater Montreal region, the Commission emphasized the need for training and integration of a workforce made up of new arrivals in industries and workplaces until now barely touched by pluralism. These measures are all the more relevant as it became abundantly clear during the Commission's regional tour that the most negative reactions to interculturalism often were expressed in locations geographically quite far from Montreal. The two co-chairs, in fact, sometimes had to listen impassively to anti-Semitic and Islamophobic remarks that are completely unacceptable in a democratic context marked by respect for differences and minority religious traditions. There is no doubt that a considerable amount of work in the area of adaptation and adjustment remains to be done among those segments of the francophone population, who until now have had minimal exposure to pluralism and who are gripped by feelings of anger and insecurity when faced with the phenomenon of immigration. This was vividly demonstrated in the unsavoury declarations made by the elected representatives of the small municipality of Hérouxville.

The Commission, however, was a lot less successful in its treatment of secularism in Québec society. It is all the more deplorable that during the consultations and in the media the place of religion in the public space seemed to provoke a vehement reaction, especially when the rights of believers gave the impression of contradicting gender equality as proclaimed in the Canadian and Québec charters. Many of the disparaging remarks regarding minority religions heard during this exercise came from individuals outraged at seeing that Muslims, Hasidic Jews, or followers of other spiritual paths were not afraid to openly declare their religious affiliations, notably when requesting the services of the state. In such a context, the co-chairs Bouchard and Taylor unfortunately appeared to be putting forward the notion that fundamental rights must be prioritized, that free expression of opinions, religious ideas, and beliefs must give way at times to other overriding legal principles, notably laïcité: 'Diversity constitutes an important value in Québec society, but it is not as fundamental as male/female equality. In a general way, it should prevail wherever possible, for example in the distribution of students in a classroom, in swimming classes, etc.'[11]

The co-chairs also affirmed on many occasions that the decisions of Canadian courts with respect to reasonable accommodation in matters of religious beliefs only applied to specific cases and not to all individuals in our society, thereby appearing to ignore the legal principle of universality that is part of Canadian federal law. This led Bouchard and Taylor to inadvisably recommend the following to the Québec government:

> As for the wearing by agents of the State of religious signs, we recommend that magistrates and Crown prosecutors, police officers, prison guards and the president and vice-president of the National Assembly be prohibited from doing so. However, we believe that all other government employees such as teachers, public servants, health professionals and so on should be authorized to wear religious signs.[12]

It is difficult to understand how the rights of one category of people, when carrying out their responsibilities within government structures, are fundamentally different from those of another group undertaking different tasks. Why would a judge of the Supreme Court of Canada or a police officer be denied a privilege in the area of freedom of expression which is granted to a university professor, a civil servant, or a physician in a hospital financed by public coffers? Furthermore, it seems incoherent to promote the fundamental right of men and women to equal treatment while refusing some of these same people the free exercise of another right inscribed in the Charter. Certainly, the proposal to write a white paper on secularism could help clarify this key question, but only on condition of disregarding the opinions of the two co-chairs on this issue.

The other great weakness of the Bouchard-Taylor Commission Report is placing responsibility for widespread diversification of this society solely on immigrants and their descendants. By doing this, the co-chairs give the impression that pluralism is a new phenomenon in Québec society and that it only affects new arrivals to the country. On this front, the commissioners seem to have forgotten that the Charter also aims to protect the rights of other groups who are victims of discrimination because of age, sexual orientation, national origin, disability, pregnancy, or vulnerability related to their religious convictions. Moreover, all individuals who are clearly identifiable as belonging to a visible minority, as members of a minority culture or belief system, or as speaking a non-official language, are not necessarily born in a foreign country or to non-Canadian parents. In wanting to direct a large portion of their recommendations towards recently arrived immigrants, including francization, recognition of diplomas, regionalization of immigration influxes, or promotion of interculturalism, the two co-chairs have forgotten that Québec diversity is also the reality of the general population. The time is long gone when the aspirations, life projects, and cultural identity of Québecers quietly followed the same model agreed to by all. Due to modernity in all its forms, globalization, the widespread use of new media, and the moral freedom enjoyed by individuals, pluralism has taken up permanent residence in our society. All these phenomena require that individuals possess an uncommon capacity for tolerance and openness.

Québec still has a lot of reflecting to do on the question of cultural diversity, especially when it presents itself in the form of external signs of a minority religion within the population. It is even more evident that Montrealers and the rest of Québecers, undoubtedly more than the residents in other large metropolitan regions of Canada, sometimes feel a deep-seated fear when faced with pluralism and multiple identities. This is a direct consequence of the historical status of the French language in the country. Nonetheless, modernity and the globalization of migratory movements knock on Québec's doors as much as anywhere else in Canada. During the next decade, because of the growing need for specialized labour and the lowering of cultural barriers all over the world, the nature of diversity in urban Québec will become increasingly complex and perhaps also unnerving. The challenge of maintaining a sphere of French expression in Montreal will probably appear to be greater to some. As well, the demands of a benevolent secularism and the necessity of maintaining a balance among the various facets of the Charter of Rights and Freedoms will require the opening of new negotiations that will perhaps be even more difficult than those currently being held.

The Bouchard-Taylor Commission, led by two intellectuals not belonging to any of the most vulnerable cultural communities and not having had a direct experience of 'reasonable accommodation' within a pluricultural institution, did not bring that much new material to the fundamental debate concerning diversity, nor did it contribute in a decisive manner to the resolution of specific difficulties. Moreover, the long public consultation sessions gave the impression that the co-chairs singularly lacked political sense, especially when hostile remarks about diversity were repeatedly heard. Ultimately, it is up to the elected representatives of all political parties to shoulder their responsibilities in this matter and show the way, in conformity with the great founding texts of our democracy. A commission, no matter how knowledgeable, cannot take the place of men and women who have received the mandate to govern from their constituents, and who have the duty to take on, in an enlightened manner, the great arbitrations within our society. At the social and political level, the real issue of diversity and of 'reasonable accommodation' is to be found in the message of the elected representatives and in the attitude towards pluralism taken by Québec institutions. This observation goes together with the recognition that in the various Montreal neighbourhoods where it really counts, interveners and ordinary people are, to this day, dealing rather well with the pluralism that surrounds them.

2 Monoculturalism versus Interculturalism in a Multicultural World

HOWARD ADELMAN

Introduction: The Hijāb[1]

Politicians engage in cover-ups all the time. One device is to use commissions as distractions, as a method for stalling or to push apparent change while allowing substantive changes to go unattended. Yet governments, in fact all Western countries, have difficulty dealing with individuals who cover their faces. Faces are masked to hide (by criminals) or to frighten (during Halloween). In some cultures, faces are sometimes covered during mourning to discourage social intercourse and encourage respect for the privacy of grieving. Normally, individuals want to read another person's face as an interpretive part of a conversation. Hence, it is no surprise that wearing a *burqa* that completely covers the whole body and veils the eyes, or a *niqab* that shows only the eyes, is controversial.[2]

However, the central artifact in this chapter is neither the burqa nor the niqab, but the hijāb, which is just a headscarf. However, it also has been interpreted as a threat, but only in a few jurisdictions.[3] The hijāb is a symbol of 'demarcation, distinction, exclusion and discrimination'[4] between Muslim and non-Muslim, between men and women, between tradition and modernity, and between acceptance and rejection (Senior 2007). Opposition to wearing the hijāb is identified in some societies with confronting a symbol of male oppression of women and extreme Islamicism. When the hijāb is banned in schools and government institutions, that ban arguably fosters commonality and reinforces a French (or German or Turkish) identity.[5] When wearing the hijāb is tolerated, as in Canada, it arguably promotes acceptance and fosters migrant integration (Eisenstadt 2007). The hijāb then becomes the symbol of that tolerance and of the underlying political culture that largely determines integration norms.

A *political* culture defines the boundaries and limits in respecting differences. What is politically legitimate in the *res publica* and how is that public space defined? Debates over the hijäb provide a window into the political character of the West and the tensions within and among different parts of Western civilization – in this chapter, between France and Québec with the rest of Canada (ROC) hovering in the background. Although focusing on the hijäb, this chapter is not about Islamic culture, but about differences among Western cultures. It is about the way we define '*Our*' culture by defining the culture of the '*Other*,' or even whether an other is defined as *other* or as just a different part of us. The *political* culture defines the boundaries and limits in respecting differences. What is politically legitimate in the res publica and how is that public space defined? Debates over the hijäb provide a window into the political culture of these two French-speaking, Western political jurisdictions, and allows the political system itself to be probed at a deeper level at the core of politics – how and under what conditions new members are to be accepted into a society.

While Joppke (2009) explores the links between headscarf controversies and Muslim integration and the rise of radical Islam, and the response as an illiberal retreat from multiculturalism (Parekh 2000), this chapter uses the conflict over the veil to interpret the controversies and the different responses in different jurisdictions more as expressions and articulations of contradictions within the domestic political cultures in the interpretation of liberalism.

This chapter is *not* about why women wear the hijäb, though women seem to wear a hijäb for a wide variety of reasons – from habit to personal faith, as a safety measure, and as a way to lure a husband.[6] However, our purpose is to use the debate to throw light on different Western approaches to difference, and not to explore whether Islam represses its women, or is evolving towards its own version of secularism (Roy 2007), or whether the state represses its Muslim minorities (Boulangé 2004).

So I am *not* ultimately concerned with why women wear the hijäb, nor about the difference between those who wear the hijäb and others who do not. I am not even focused on assessing degrees of permissiveness. Rather, this chapter is about how different societies, specifically those of France and Québec, respond politically to women wearing that form of headscarf. Different political cultures in each society offer a partial explanation for the different ways the problem of difference in general and the hijāb issue in particular are handled. The controversies over the hijāb allow us to explore the different political cultures of France and Québec, specifically in relationship to how each culture politically handles the issue of difference.[7] The Stasi and the Bouchard-Taylor commissions offer us two doorways into that exploration.

France and the Stasi Commission

Context

At the beginning of the twentieth century, when France was overwhelmingly Catholic (practising or lapsed), with a small Protestant minority of approximately 2 per cent and an even tinier Jewish presence one-tenth that size,[8] France was steeped in the politics of head coverings. The original 1905 effort to ban the 'habit' targeted the power of the Catholic Church, which at the time was a prime supporter of reactionary politics. Ethnic myths, historical memories, symbols, and traditions play crucial roles in the creation and maintenance of the collective identity of modern nations. France is certainly no exception. Its antipathy to the habit is part of its essentialist creed.

In the last 20 years, head coverings once again became an issue, this time in response to Islam rather than Catholicism. When two sisters and a cousin – Fatima, Leila, and Samira – were expelled from a school in the small town of Créiteil outside Paris in 1989, *l'affaire du foulard* (the scarf affair) broke into the open. A French high court determined that religious insignia *could* be worn in state schools[9] (Godfrey 2003). The hijāb was deemed *not* to be incompatible with la laïcité as long as the purpose of the accessory was *not* intended to pursue the four p's: 'pressure, provocation, proselytism or propaganda.'[10] For laïcité was based on freedom of conscience, separation of church and state, and the neutrality of the state in dealing with any religion. The initial legal response supported the rights of Muslim girls to wear the hijāb. Within five years of that ruling, the total number of girls wearing headscarves in school rose from 10 children to almost 2,000 out of 1.8 million Muslim school girls (McGoldrick 2006: 256). Ten years later, by 2004, that number had declined to 1,256 (Keaton 2006: 181).[11]

For critics, the hijāb is an identity marker for oppression and inequality of women under Islam. Ardent feminists, who uphold the tradition of equal rights for all, regard the foulard as a symbol of paternalism, of patriarchy, of Muslim male oppression of women (*la femme soumise*), a means to control women's bodies and identities, and as a symbol of legitimizing violence against women. Muslim fathers and brothers allegedly pressure girls to wear the hijäb in schools as an effective instrument of control (Beaud and Pialoux 2003; Maruani 2009). Muslim girls who do not wear the hijäb are in turn accused of being loose or even called whores.

Gang rapes (*tournantes*) brought the issue to the fore once again. Samira Bellil, a French feminist originally raised as a Muslim, published an autobiography, *Dans l'enfer des tournantes* (In the hell of the gang rapes[12]), in 2002. She described the sexual abuse and rapes that she and other young Muslim girls endured in the *banlieues*, the suburbs of Paris and other French cities. She herself was first gang-raped at the age of 14. Though gang rapes had taken place well before the immigrants arrived, and although the Parisian newspaper *Libération* found that 27 of 29 recent gang-rape cases had been committed by non-immigrant men (Bowen 2003: 214–16), there was a widespread belief that most gang rapes by Muslim youth were not being reported.[13]

Against this background, one event brought the issue to the fore once again, and set the match to the anti-hijäb torch that many thought had been extinguished by the 1989 court ruling – the burning of a 17-year-old girl, Sohane, on 4 October 2002, by a Muslim male youth in Vitry. The murdered girl's sister created NPNS, *Ni Putes Ni Soumises* (Neither Whores Nor Doormats) to counter the oppression of Muslim women, of which the hijäb was the symbol. The Iranian writer Djavann Chahdortt (2003) threw the pages of her vitriolic campaign against the symbolism of the veil in her *Bas les voiles*, and helped create a firestorm.[14]

On 3 July 2003, Jacques Chirac, the French president, called on Bernard Stasi, the French ombudsman (*médiateur de la République*) and expert on immigration, to head up a 20-member commission that included intellectuals (the philosopher and former communist Régis Debray, and the sociologist Alain Touraine), academic experts on immigration (Patrick Weil and Jacqueline Costa-Lascoux), religious leaders (Cardinal Lustiger, Mohamed Arkoun, and Gilles Kepel), politicians (Michel Delebarre, deputy-mayor of Dunkirk; and Nicole Guedj, a municipal councillor in Pantin, an inner-Parisian suburb), a school principal (Ghislaine Hudson), a rights mediator (Hanifa Cherifi, a secular Muslim who tried to persuade girls who had been expelled for wearing a hijäb to stop wearing it and return to school), and a representative from *Ni Putes Ni Soumises*. The Stasi Commission was set up to look into whether the hijāb was a possible threat to la laïcité. Most of those appointed already believed that to be the case.

After conducting over 100 interviews and receiving several thousand submissions, on 11 December 2003 the Stasi Commission delivered its report, the Independent Commission of Reflection on the Application of the Principle of *Laïcité*.[15] Among its many recommendations, many addressing the horrible situation of the French suburbs, the Commission recommended a ban on the wearing of conspicuous religious symbols in schools, which, along with the recommendation of holidays for religious feast days, required a change in the law.[16]

The Political and Intellectual Debate

The magazine *Elle* depicted *un voile* as symbolizing 'intolerable discrimination.' Sixty prominent women in the Association femmes publiques, in December 2003, supported the ban against 'this visible symbol of the submission of women in public.'[17] In France a majority supported banning headscarves worn by a tiny group of young female teenagers. Intellectuals became involved in the debate. Paul Ricoeur (2004), one of France's leading philosophers, opposed penalizing girls who wore a hijāb by expulsion because that would deny the girls their only access to freedom. He offered other reasons for convincing girls not to wear the headscarf by considering the headscarves not as religious symbols, but as threats to the role of schools in the republic of indoctrinating students in la laïcité. Further, in encouraging the girls to engage in dialogue, Ricoeur insisted that in order to resolve the matter through dialogue, the girls first had to engage in and commit themselves to la laïcite as a condition of attending public schools and establishing parity and mutual respect.

Ricoeur (2004) grounds ethics in culture and within a historical narrative and continuing institutions. His communitarian thesis is based on assimilation of the Other into French culture and its secular religion of French republicanism grounded in la laïcité. When he, like Habermas (1991) in Germany, articulated different philosophical grounds for the necessity of a contextualized res publica in which the self is mediated by its relationship to another, Ricoeur tried to lift discourse above subjective prejudices into the arena of rationality on an ethical plane where a loving self was concerned about the well-being of the other, an unequal other in terms of power, and where both the receiver of assistance and the giver recognize the fragility of life and their mutual commitment to improving its quality by achieving the good life. For Ricoeur, they must do so in a context in which each belongs to a community with its own historical collective narrative that sustains human speech and action and requires institutional reinforcing mechanisms.

A year before he died, in his 2004 essay written with Monique Canto-Serber, Ricoeur claimed that the proper interpretation of la laïcité ruled out exclusion.[18] For Ricoeur, la laïcité insists that the other be solicited to join and be assimilated into the dominant French culture and not be coerced, so that the initiative to do so depends on the solicited accepting the goodwill of the French society soliciting them to join. But la laïcité also requires accepting the terms of that assimilation – the surrender of any cultural accretions in public spaces that are interpreted by the solicitors of France as running contrary to the secular religion of France as found in its culture and institutions and encapsulated by la laïcité (Pena-Ruiz 2005). So one axis of the debate focused on whether the hijäb was to be excluded from the public schools by persuasion or legal coercion.

The leftist critics also threw doubt on the motives of the conservative government of France. Boulangé (2004) suggested racism motivated the attack, while others suggested that the conservative element of the French Muslim community was only an ostensible target and that the 'secularist' campaign was ultimately aimed at the working class in general and at the union of teachers and students who opposed the ban. In the name of preserving the ideal of French education as a republican one, they argued that the real intent was to dismantle the national education system. The whole hijäb debate was simply an exercise in distraction and dissimulation, a magician's trick in disorientation ostensibly in defence of political freedom to recall and replay revolutionary origins and ideals. Historically, banning the traditional head covering of nuns in schools in public was a left-wing trope (Leoussi and Grosby 2007). However, in 2005, in the name of an inherited tradition of revolution, banning hijäb head coverings in the public realm to conserve la laïcité was defended. In this axis of debate, the issue was government motive – dissimulation or a genuine concern with the foundations of the French state.

There was a third and probably more central axis of debate over individual liberty. North American critics such as Barnett and Duvall (2005), Carens (2005), McGoldrick (2006), Scott (2007), and Winter (2008) focused on individual rights interpreted as the right of the individual to be free of state interference. Defenders of the French action, such as Laborde (2006, 2008)[19] and Weil (2009), insisted that the state had to ban the hijäb to protect the individual rights of schoolgirls to make independent choices against a background of ostensible pressures from fathers and brothers. This debate stood against a fourth axis of debate that stood in the background, the threat of Islamic fundamentalism on the international stage, which became an explicit part of Laborde's case and was a central focus for Eisenstadt (2007), Gresh (2004a, b), and Hurd (2008).

Thus, the political debate was *not* just over banning the hijāb in schools, but over the definition of individual rights and liberties and the role of the state in threatening or protecting those rights, over the international threat of Islamism, and over whether the ban should be legislated and backed up by the force of law or whether persuasion should be used. The debate was also over the motives for undertaking a ban and whether it was a front for privatization of public schools and really an attack on the role of public education in ensuring la laïcité. Finally, it was also a debate over process in Benhabib (2004): whether the discourse had properly been conducted in arriving at a decision, which she supported; or whether adequate attention had been paid to empirical facts in making the case (Keaton 2006). Linking all these various dimensions was the issue of identity politics and how its various strands were to be knitted together.

Results

Whatever the different weights given to the various rationales and critiques, the concrete aftermath of the legislation and the intellectual debates that still continue were very clear. Following the recommendations of the Stasi Report, French legislation in 2004 banned wearing 'ostentatious' religious symbols in public schools in the name of French republicanism and secularism – la laïcité.[20]

Most Muslim citizens, as well as most French citizens, supported the ban and its premise: fostering a French uni-culture. Polls in 2003 showed that 78 per cent of Muslims favoured la laïcité (McGoldrick 2006: 253). After the new legislation took effect, on 15 March 2004, and went into practice in the schools in September, there were 48 school expulsions that year, 45 involving the hijāb and three related to Sikh turbans.[21] On the other hand, when the Commission was announced a December 2003 survey of Muslims announced that 69 per cent were in favour of both the Commission and a ban, and only 29 per cent were opposed. Support even *increased* by almost 10 per cent when the report came out. However, when the only recommendation really taken up was the headscarf ban, and the other recommendations on making changes to enhance the opportunities for alienated youth in the suburbs were ignored, support by Muslims for the ban on wearing religious symbols in schools dropped to 42 per cent. A majority (53 per cent) were then opposed.[22]

The metaphorical rhetorical bonfire that took place in 2003 became real fires in 2005. Triggered by the electrocution of two youths who had fled to an electric substation to escape police whom they believed were pursuing them, uncoordinated riots by neighbourhood gangs[23] that began on 27 October 2005 in Clichy-sous-Bois by alienated youth then spread over the next three weeks into other destitute neighbourhoods, the 'cités,' or *'quartiers difficiles.'* Almost 9,000 vehicles were torched; dozens of buildings, such as a junior high school in Grenoble, were set on fire; 126 police and firefighters were injured; and one bystander was killed. The losses were estimated at about $300 million. However, that had a great deal to do with unemployment, despair, and possibly discrimination, but nothing to do with displays of religious identity. The importance of these events, for our purposes, is that government acted swiftly and precisely concerning the ostentatious display of religious symbols on school kids, but ignored the more substantive issue of the plight of unemployed youth in the suburbs.

Québec and the Bouchard-Taylor Commission

Context

Fifty years after la laïcité had become the foundation of secularism in France, Québec underwent its own Quiet Revolution to reject the dominant position of the Catholic Church. Further, to retain its status as a linguistic collective identity, Québec passed legislation that insisted new immigrants be assimilated into the French majority in the province (see chapter 1). The challenge for accomplishing that was compounded by misperceptions and politics. Of 73 cases of cultural conflict examined over 23 years, there were only 13 cases in the first 16 years, 12 cases in the next four years, but 40 in the third phase, the Time of Turmoil, that led to the creation of Québec's B-T Commission. The issue became a matter of public debate, broadening from minority religious and cultural practices to integration of immigrants and minorities. The extreme case of Hérouxville (mentioned in the Introduction and in chapter 1) ran counter to that effort. At the other end of the spectrum, in 2006 the Superior Court of Québec permitted Sikh youth to wear a kirpan in school. On the other hand, while Ontario's female hockey players could wear a hijäb, in Québec a Muslim referee said they could not. In January 2007, the Action démocratique du Québec (ADQ), in a widely reported letter, denounced the Québéquois' surrender to minorities, and 'reasonable accommodation' began to accrue negative connotations.

In 2005 and 2006, a series of media stories, some depicted in the Introduction, played up tensions arising from the *appearance* of religious symbols in public or the effects of non-Christian religious practices on others. Muslims asked for space to pray in a restaurant, and a large room was evacuated for a short time to accommodate them. Special requests were allegedly made to government employees to protect religious sensibilities and practices, such as providing female driving-test officers for Muslim women. Two non-Jewish visitors to a Jewish hospital were evidently prevented from eating ham sandwiches.

In Québec, Mario Dumont's ADQ had leaped from a marginal party to become the second strongest party in the province in the 2007 elections, ahead of the separatist Parti Québécois, in part by attacking the application of reasonable accommodation for cultural minorities. The implication: the generosity of Québécois to cultural minorities was being abused. The election resulted in the first minority parliament in over a century of politics in that province.[24] Mario Dumont had been dubbed Québec's Jean-Marie Le Pen for his exploitation of a backlash against Muslims and the debate over reasonable accommodation to the social and cultural practices of minorities.[25] Premier Jean Charest's support for the expulsion of the young girl from the soccer tournament for wearing a hijäb was widely believed to be a response to the newly perceived threat from the right.[26] So was his announcement in February 2007 that he was creating what became known as the B-T Commission. A world renowned philosopher and totally bilingual federalist anglophone, Charles Taylor (see Notes, Introduction, n4), who was born in and has retained a lifelong commitment to Québec; and a very highly regarded Québécois sociologist, separatist, and brother of a former leader of the Parti Québécois, Gérard Bouchard (see n3), were appointed to head the Commission.

Process

While the Stasi Commission had a narrow focus – the wearing of conspicuous symbols of religious affiliation in public schools – and a baseline to provide guidance, namely laïcité, the Bouchard-Taylor Commission had a much wider compass – the issue of diversity in general. Its reference point was also far more general: the core values of Québec as a *pluralistic*, *democratic*, and *egalitarian* society. While Stasi sought appropriate governing principles, B-T was charged with looking into *practices* in handling diversity, not only in Québec society but elsewhere as well. Both commissions engaged in a broad process of consultation, but B-T went further in holding public hearings across the province and televising them, giving wide play to individuals to grandstand and offer very intolerant views in contrast to the organizational presentations that dominated Stasi. Both commissions were asked to make recommendations, both legal and otherwise. For Stasi, non-legal recommendations meant general political policies to help end the alienation of youth. For B-T, non-legal recommendations meant small adjustments to government policies and respect for the practices of reasonable accommodation in civil society.

The Debate

As in many things Canadian, differences are often linguistic, not in just the narrow sense but in the connotations and associations of words and phrases. (See the discussion concerning *accommodement raisonnable* in French and 'reasonable accommodation' in English in the Introduction.) In French, *accommodement* is associated with compromise; in English, if someone said the accommodation was reasonable, they would mean not great but not bad either. So when *accommodement raisonnable* is translated into English, it tends to be associated with modest improvements or changes by a host community to satisfy a guest. In other words, it refers to changes by the existing society to adjust to and satisfy a different community. In turn, these associations also become attached to *accommodement raisonnable* in Québec.

Empirical Analysis

In the media coverage, B-T documented only six of 21 cases that were accurately reported. In the other 15 cases, there were striking distortions which correlated with negative public misperceptions.[27] B-T offered a number of examples:

- The widespread misperception that men who accompanied spouses to prenatal classes offered by CLSC de Parc-Extension were excluded from a course at the request of Muslim women. This was false; CLSC

de Parc-Extension daytime programs, including prenatal lessons, were attended by men. There were two evening prenatal courses exclusively for expectant Muslim mothers.
- A widespread misperception that the management of the Société de l'assurance automobile du Québec (SAAQ) had ordered its female driving examiners to yield to male colleagues when Orthodox Jews take driving tests was false; SAAQ did provide female driving examiners for female Muslim women if one was available, and, if not, allowed the test to be rescheduled, but not at the expense of gender equality, infringement of public order, or safety of premises or individuals.
- It was widely reported that Muslims had demanded that the Mont-Saint-Grégoire 'sugarhouse' restaurant's menu conform to their standards, and that other patrons had been expelled so that Muslim patrons could say prayers; in fact, a modified menu that excluded pork and included halal sausage and salami provided by Astrolabe, a Muslim association, had been arranged a week in advance. Further, the Muslim association had reserved one of four dining halls for its exclusive use, and when they moved tables to pray, management, in its anxiety to get the room back since the restaurant was very busy, stopped the music for the 30 girls present for 10 minutes in a dance hall accommodating 650 so the men could pray.
- In another widely misreported case, food was ostensibly modified at a cost of tens of millions of dollars to earn a kosher label; in reality, the kosher label was a marketing strategy targeting the U.S. market at minimal additional cost with no modification of ingredients.
- Nurses from CLSC Thérèse-de-Blainville, who provided home health care for patients in the Boisbriand Hasidic community, were purportedly forced to comply with the Hasidic dress code; in reality, only 1.7 per cent of the clients served by CLSC TdeB and the home care services were Hasidic, and services to that community constituted only 0.1 per cent of all home health care; the health care workers were not subjected to a dress code.

Results

The Bouchard-Taylor Commission was created under very different circumstances and proposed radically different policies. However, there were two clear similarities. Both societies had a commitment to gender equality, and both were committed to the promotion of French language and culture, although there were differences in how the Stasi Commission interpreted French culture and how B-T did. The Stasi Commission Report had been written and published several years before Bouchard and Taylor began their work. In reading B-T, the Stasi Commission seems to have served as a foil. The B-T Report openly criticized France's restrictive legislation concerning the wearing of religious signs in public schools. B-T did not agree with excluding certain forms of religious expression in the public sphere (B-T Report, abridged, 45), including the prohibition against state civil servants wearing religious signs in public.

Secondly, for France, neutrality of the state was not simply a mechanism but an ultimate purpose; secularism was an *essential* component of the republic's identity. While France prohibited religious accommodation under the principle of the neutrality of the state, B-T found prohibition to be incompatible with state neutrality and interculturalism. Third, Stasi did not link institutional structures *in civil society* to the purposes of secularism (Stasi, 46). In contrast, the open secularism advocated in B-T linked the final purposes of secularism (principles 1 and 2) to institutional structures (3 and 4) so that practices were embedded in social institutions. Fourth, education in France had an emancipatory mission *directed against religion*; the B-T Report did not find this to be compatible with the principle of state neutrality in respect of religion and non-religion. Finally, and most characteristically, whereas in France integration was viewed as assimilation into an existing dominant culture, in the B-T Report the integration process in a diversified society was to be achieved through exchanges *between* citizens who come to know and understand one another – hence, Québec interculturalism as distinct from French uniculturalism and English Canadian multiculturalism, which, the B-T Report suggests, in common with the French practice, relegates minority identities to the background in the public realm.

In Québec, the headscarf was one of a number of issues that led to the Bouchard-Taylor commission report that endorsed the doctrine of interculturalism to distinguish the Québec approach from both the monoculturalism of France and the multiculturalism[28] of the rest of Canada (ROC) (Ruby 2003). France and French and English Canada each responded quite differently to the hijäb issue. The different responses throw light on the distinct political cultures of English Canada and the two French-speaking polities, one of which, France, has almost as many Muslims as there are French speakers in Québec.

In Québec, in an interview in the *Journal de Montréal*, former sovereignist premier Jacques Parizeau called the Bouchard-Taylor Report on reasonable accommodation 'long and boring.' Parizeau criticized the report for putting French Canadians on trial even though the sociologist Gérard Bouchard had been a declared sovereignist for 40 years. He was a typical Québec sociologist obsessed with the nationalist question (Fournier 2002). However, Bouchard rejected the notions of the pre-Second World War early sociologists in Québec; they had portrayed the francophone difference as a handicap (Fournier 2001). Bouchard belonged to the 'civic nation' rather than the 'ethnic nation' view of Québec society. Further, though Bouchard was trained at the Université Laval and the Université de Paris at Nanterre, he has always been involved with a number of deeply empirical and historical studies, including the study of hereditary and genetic diseases, applied genetics, rural Québec history, and – his work since 2002 – the Québec imaginary. He has been involved as well with research on anti-racism with Michèle Lamont of Harvard University. In contrast, Alain Tourraine, the pre-eminent sociologist on the Stasi Commission, was far less an empiricist, had invented the conception of post-industrialization, and was more concerned with social movements in general.

Critics of the B-T Report complained that the recommendations demanded that old-stock Québecers accommodate immigrants rather than the other way around. Parti Québécois leader Pauline Marois was disappointed that the Commission did not propose enshrining the 'common values' of Québecers in legislation as her proposed Québec Identity Act would have done, requiring new immigrants to demonstrate a minimal command of French to become citizens of Québec or to be eligible to participate in the political life of Québec. Québec judges would have to weigh the historical heritage and fundamental values of the Québec nation in their rulings. Thus, the state and the laws of the land in Québec had not, according to the critics, protected the history and the majority culture of French Canada. For conservatives, even in the guise of revolutionary separatists, the state was obligated to protect the national cultural heritage. When the B-T Report first emerged, Premier Jean Charest, on 22 May 2008, immediately dismissed the recommendation of the report to remove the cross from the legislative chamber with the words, 'We cannot erase our history,' which was perhaps a harbinger of decisions to come.

Comparing the Two Commissions of Inquiry

The two commissions had radically different mandates: to defend la laïcité in France and to clarify the meaning and application of reasonable accommodation in Québec. Laïcité was both an ideal and a fundamental foundation stone and initial starting position. In contrast, reasonable accommodation is a dynamic process constantly underway. The two commissions also faced radically different circumstances. In France, there was a real crisis, which the Stasi Commission recognized and which the government ignored, and, in Québec, an apparent crisis, stimulated by the media and the government, which the Commission understood. Further, the processes were starkly different in important respects. Although both commissions conducted numerous public hearings, the French Commission never once interviewed or gathered the empirical data to learn why the girls had chosen to wear the hijāb. In contrast, the B-T Commission investigated and reported in great detail the circumstances that had given rise to the stories of reported cultural conflict, undermining the myths. The conclusions were also radically different. Stasi thought that the girls needed to become more flexible and *required* by law to accommodate to the fundamental doctrine of laïcité, lest Islamicism gain a foothold and to prevent family coercion. B-T thought that the state and its institutions should become more flexible and allow civil society to sort out problems. The results were also radically different. B-T was totally ignored and even dismissed and degraded. Stasi was honoured and accepted, but only with respect to appearances and not material substance.

The Stasi Commission Report justified the use of state authority to dictate external public appearance; B-T, in the English philosophical tradition, sought to reconcile state authority and individual liberty and limit the reach of the former to the benefit of the latter. The Bouchard-Taylor Report was steeped in empirical sociology; the Stasi Commission came from a tradition of deducing results from abstract principles and concepts.

For B-T, legislating against wearing religious symbols specifically, or the conduct of religious practices more generally, was *not* an appropriate area of government intervention for it undermined the proper duty of governmental authority to remain neutral in matters of both religious belief and practice. The function of the magistrate was not to prescribe particular policies but to secure the civil interest of citizens. Law provides a legal framework within which contentious social problems can be resolved primarily in civil society. According to B-T, Québec offered proof that it excelled in the practice of tolerance. Further, it did so because Québecers, though not the Québec media, were blessed with a second virtue, reasonableness. In France, magisterial authority determined and adjudicated the public space instead of letting civil society find the answers within reasonable boundaries. B-T demonstrated that Québec civil society possessed those virtues in abundance and did not require the heavy hand of the state or France's idea of magisterial authority.

B-T went further. Taylor proposed an *exercise* concept of freedom that embodied both negative freedom as an absence of interference, and a positive notion of freedom possessed by all humans that reformulated the Québec notion of *maître chez nous* as a capacity for self-mastery, self-rule, and self-direction exercised not by the state or the body politic but by all members of civil society. Québec had already achieved Cécile Laborde's goal of self-empowerment entailed in her critical republicanism (Laborde 2008) without the heavy hand of the state as exemplified in French republicanism. Civil society was not merely the realm of negative freedom, but the opportunity for every member of a society to exercise not only his/her own beliefs and habits in the public sphere without any unreasonable interference in the lives of others, but to understand and sympathize with the practices of *les autres*. Québec civil society was already well on the way to achieving the highest plane of freedom, and did not require the helping hand of the state. In case after case, B-T demonstrated that Québecers were quite capable of making fine discriminations among different options, and recognizing reasonable limitations on freedom that fostered mutual appreciation and understanding based on a respect for human equality and individual and community freedom of self-expression. In France, an active state, primarily in the school system, was a prerequisite to turning out French citizens.

Secularism was also the ideal in Québec after the Quiet Revolution. Paradoxically, Québec advocated reasonable accommodation, but the language laws and the language police, the instruments of state authority and upholders of 'the tradition,' were often quite unreasonable in their edicts and rulings. Yet Québecers, in their actions and in their deeds in civil society, demonstrated a wide range of sweet reasonableness. While accommodation was perceived widely as surrender of the French tradition in Québec to the threats of different cultures, ordinary Québecers adopted the very opposite meaning of accommodation, adjusting easily to circumstances and to 'others.' For accommodation included a broad set of equivocal meanings, all bearing a family resemblance but taking on very opposed conceptions in the extreme interpretations – from selling out received truths by granting privileges to minorities, to adjusting to the realities on the ground.

In contrast to France, the issue of the hijāb did not preoccupy Québecers, but a widespread misperception had arisen that Québecers had bent over much too far to accommodate minorities. Unlike the Stasi Commission Report in France, which enjoyed wide support, the B-T Report was widely maligned. Had the report revealed the dark underside of the Québec sovereignist movement as an effort to preserve a traditional Québec monoculture and the historical heritage of the Québec nation – quite different than France's la laïcité – it would undoubtedly have been reviled even more. There remained a non-rational core in Québec's view of 'reasonable' and 'accommodation' as further expressions of the long process of surrender of a colonized people to the dominance of English culture, in spite of the overt meaning of the phrase.

The Stasi Report can be read in counterpoint to America as well as a domestic expression, in that the objective for newcomers was total assimilation. Both France and the United States uphold a radical separation of church and state, though for very opposite reasons – to free the individual from the long arm of religion in the public sphere in France, and to allow a variety of religious expression in the public sphere for Americans. In contrast, B-T can be read as a counterpoint to English Canada, especially since B-T went out of the way to contrast interculturalism as a higher plane of tolerance and understanding versus multiculturalism.

La laïcité is not only a legal norm in France for denying certain types of acts. Laïcité also requires a positive inculcation of values by schools as the *singular* tool for teaching the values of French citizenship by a finely crafted common-culture curriculum intended to bind young republicans morally and civically to their homeland. Jules Ferry, the nineteenth-century educational godfather of la laïcité, believed that scientific method and rational thought would replace religious exegesis as the backbone of the French educational system. Religious neutrality requires exclusion of any competing values originating in religious sources that appear to threaten republican values. Yet in linking French republicanism and positivism in a symbiotic marriage, the result reflects a top-down paternalistic approach akin to the Catholic Church, to which it ostensibly stands in opposition.

In France, citizens cannot behave *culturally* different as *public persons* (as distinct from differently in public) yet be equally French (Bowen 2003, 247). 'Acceptable progress in the school system is measured not only by the acquisition of knowledge, but additionally by a student's capacity to assimilate the dominant behavioural forms and cultural norms that are presented to them as their own' (Keaton 2006, 97). Through schooling, the state displaces the family as the instrument for educating and supervising the ethical value development of the individual. The inculcation of knowledge and norms becomes the vehicle ostensibly for producing a cooperative and compliant citizenry instead of putting the primary stress on ensuring that each individual in society has the means and opportunities to succeed. Most French reject multiculturalism, reject that there are different beliefs, norms, and practices that can be both publicly displayed and tolerated within public (state-controlled) space, indeed respected, and cause no harm to anyone else, *or to the national polity.*

In the contemporary context, the headscarf issue was also connected with the failure to integrate second- and third-generation descendents of North African, West African, and Turkish immigrants (Sorensen 1996). The outer suburbs of French cities bear an eerie parallel with the inner cities of America, with high youth unemployment rates and declining unemployment benefits, deteriorating public housing, and declining social services and spending on health. The preponderantly Muslim underclass belied France's ostensible celebration of equality. The Stasi Commission documented that inequality in spite of France's tradition of upholding *egalité* as one of its highest values; the French government initially ignored the equality recommendations.

The issue of disenchanted youth who mostly happen to be Muslim is of central concern to France, both as a matter of international relations and as a domestic issue. This failure of French education and immigrant integration (Lorcerie 2001) was more often viewed as a deficiency in the culture of its immigrant population (Keaton 2006: 194). Since the Muslim population of France was generally fluent in French, the focus shifted to Islam, a focus reinforced by France's relations with its former colonies in North Africa as well as by international terrorism (Hurd 2008: 1). France experienced a 'clash of civilizations' involving 'an historic reaction of an ancient rival against our Judeo-Christian heritage, our secular present, and the worldwide expansion of both,' even though academics such as Roy had already traced the problems to the failure of integration (Lewis 2003).

How could the state deny high-school girls the right to choose to wear a kerchief, *un foulard*, on their head, if the decision was made on their own without pressure and in opposition to the rulings of a paternalist state and its civil servants, especially in a society where the tradition of rights and the achievement of gender equality had been hard-fought battles? How could one explain that leading French feminists opposed giving the right to teenage girls who chose to wear a hijāb?

The explanation involves a complex interweaving of different factors. A central pillar of French values is the concept of *droit*, the equality of rights *guaranteed by the state*, currently focused primarily on the equality of the sexes. That equality was a product of a hard struggle with the Catholic Church, which had placed women in subordinate roles and resisted liberal divorce laws and abortion rights. The historical struggle of women to obtain the freedom to uncover increasing aspects of their bodies in public symbolized the core of French values and la laïcité. Secondly, secularism was the ideal of France. Holding on to one's heritage but adapting to France was the most common immigrant integration strategy.

Secularism, la laïcité, was a source of political authority in its own right, reified through public debates, defining policies, and providing justifications for those policies. Public figures defined the relationship of religion and the state to one another and both to the individual in the politics of public reasoning. Caught in the crosscurrents of the publicly espoused religion of secularism and the private teachings of family that taught religion as entailing behaviour that encompassed public life, girls were caught between the oppressive weight of their own paternalistic heritage and the paternalism of the state, which, in the name of a 'common culture,' taught that diversity was to be ignored. These women were excluded socially by the synergistic effects of their paternalist upbringing and the detached 'universal' ideals of the state, which ignored the history of colonialism and decolonization (Keaton 2006: 124–5). The explicit function of the French national educational system was the reproduction and transmission of a unitary and irreducible common culture (Keaton 2006:10; Bowen 2003, 32; McGoldrick 2006: 39). French culture did not entail understanding and explaining the reality that its citizens were, in fact, products of many cultures and diverse histories. French political thinkers relied on the generalities of law to iron out these paradoxes and contradictions.

Secularism in France was dedicated to preserving the supremacy of Abstract Reason – Reason with a capital 'R' – that since Descartes has highly valued clear and distinct ideas and first principles and the use of deductive reasoning in applying those principles, rather than dealing with messy reality through the use of fuzzy rather than syllogistic logic in a time of caprice and uncertainty.

Seyla Benhabib (2004) argued that the state failed to observe the principle of accountability, but that if the girls had been heard, 'it would have become clear that the meaning of wearing the scarf itself was changing from being a religious act to one of cultural defiance and increasing politicization' (191). It was unclear how she could know that, since the girls never had a chance to explain their actions. Nevertheless, Benhabib argued that the failure to allow the girls to speak and be interrogated essentially re-imprisoned the three girls 'within the walls of patriarchal meaning,' and contradicted French norms of respect and equal treatment for religious beliefs that required that they be allowed to 'clarify how they intend to treat the beliefs of others from different religions' (192).

Keaton did hear girls explain why they wore the hijāb when she interviewed Muslim girls in a middle school, a multi-track high school, and a vocational school in Pantin outside Paris between 1995 and 2005. The girls were thoughtful and articulate and said they chose to wear the hijāb to bring them closer to God and/or their culture as they negotiated how to both preserve and transform their lives in the context of the dominant structures of power and privilege. They had *not* been pressured to wear the hijāb. They had *not* donned the hijāb as an act of rebellion. Nevertheless, French officials and many if not most intellectuals viewed wearing the hijāb as an act of defiance (Levy 2004). Although the debate within the larger context of Europe emphasized human rights, as Anne Norton (2004) commented, that abstraction denied context and the recognition of the social reality, social institutions, sociohistorical forces, and human activity that produce a structured system of material and symbolic relations. Television exacerbated the problems. While voices told them what they should be and how they should behave, Muslim youth were not represented on TV.

When lower concrete existence has been reduced to an inconspicuous moment, when what used to be important has become but a trace, a pattern shrouded in a mere shadowy outline (Hegel 1977: §28, 16); when a debate over 'habits' re-emerges from the shadows and comes out into the open; when what teenagers wear in everyday life become conspicuous and a matter of national and international debate; when the most vocal opponents of the ban turn out to be two Muslim girls named Lévy (2004), whose father is a Jewish descendent of an ancient Hebrew priestly tribe and a professed atheist; then we know we are watching a Punch and Judy show rather than a serious debate about the res publica and the polity, an interpretation in which the debate is about a piece of fabric used to hide and cover, where the wearer of that covering holds such covering-up to be an act of modesty and an expression of a link to God or overseas cultural traditions rather than as an exercise in self-expression. The irony is doubled when those who want to ban the cover-up do so in the name of upholding an original revelation of the defence of liberty, of freedom of expression that in reality is an exercise in covering up a domestic mode of colonization.

Category	Stasi	B-T
Mandate	Reconcile hijāb in schools with laïcité	Clarify 'reasonable accommodation'
Circumstances	Gang rapes and burning	Minor conflicts
Focus	Compliance with principles	Compliance with practices
Process	Consultative	Even more consultative
Media	Media and report in accord	B-T uses but criticizes media
Conclusions	Legislate ban on hijāb	Protect civil society space
Results	Adopted re appearances	Rejected
	Ignored re substance	Abused
State Authority	Esteemed	Limited
Highest value	Individual Liberty	Mutual recognition
Individual rights	Protected by state	Protected by state
Communitarianism	Ideal	Inheritance
Rationalism vs Empiricism	Rationalism	Empiricism
Ends	Legislate	Leave to civil society
Church/State	State ostensibly neutral	Neutrality of state proposed but rejected
Political Ideal	republican	democratic
State Function	Protector of individual rights	Individual rights vs. state

Conclusions

The insistence on debate, on challenges to court rulings, on commissions, on referenda, avoided the urgency of determining what had really unfolded and been revealed over two decades. In the early 1970s, following the 1968 student protests, there was a strong French reaction to dismembering the bureaucratic educational uniformity requirements. The 1986 legislation in France once again emphasized the role of education in defining French national identity. Banning the hijāb was the culminating symbol of this historical reversal.

The Québec government, on the other hand, had great difficulty in reconciling their new-found civic religion with the need to preserve their inherited traditions and values, intertwined with the preservation of the French language, particularly when faced with a loss of power. Most Québécois living cheek by jowl with minorities had no such difficulty in practising reasonable accommodation.

	Institution		Individual
Indulgent	Sufficiently tensile	Sufficiently bending	Unbending

The adjective 'tolerant' can mean indulgent, bending too much towards the other. It can also mean an ability to bear and adjust even to that which may initially be distasteful, to tolerate large pressures as in a building constructed to withstand an earthquake. These are two radically different meanings, but they are not opposites. As indicated on the above chart, they are just two distal points on one side of a scale. The opposite of too much bending is to be unbending. But it can also mean not bending sufficiently; French school girls had to learn to be more tolerant when dealing with the state and in accepting laïcité as the fundamental French creed as France saw it. Outsiders thought it was the state and its institutions that had to be more flexible. Where is the balancing point on the fulcrum where an individual retains his or her identity as one accommodates differences, and where the institutions of the state are flexible enough to adjust to the forces of change?

3 The Bouchard-Taylor Commission and the Jewish Community of Québec in Historical Perspective

IRA ROBINSON

Introduction

In the past two years, issues respecting cultural and religious diversity and its challenges have been the focus of considerable interest in Québec, as well as in the rest of Canada, due to the activities of the Bouchard-Taylor Commission. This commission, appointed by the Government of Québec to investigate the issue of 'reasonable accommodation' of cultural minorities in Québec society, has necessarily had an important impact on Québec society as a whole, and, not least, on its Jewish community.

This chapter analyses the impact of the Bouchard-Taylor Commission on the Jewish community of Québec, and contextualizes this impact with respect to the 250-year-long interaction between Québec's Jewish minority and its French Canadian majority. Since the Jewish community in Québec is long established, and since there is a relatively long history of Québecers engaged in extensive public discussions concerning the nature and desirability of the presence of a Jewish community in the province of Québec (Langlais and Rome 1995; Anctil, Robinson, and Bouchard 2000), it is possible to examine the debate in Québec surrounding the Bouchard-Taylor Commission with a historical perspective. This will be done largely in the conclusion of this chapter. Thus, it may be possible to provide a comparative examination of how and why some issues have changed and others have essentially remained in dispute, from the early and mid-twentieth century to the beginning of the twenty-first century.

While reporting fully on the events of the Commission as it affected the Jewish community, this chapter will attempt to address the following questions:

- If the Québec Jewish community is indeed hundreds of years old, why is it implicated so strongly in Québec public opinion with newly arrived immigrant communities?
- How does the anti-immigrant and anti-Jewish sentiment, which came into public view because of the Commission hearings, differ from the anti-Semitism in Québec in the early twentieth century?

'Reasonable Accommodation'

The concept of 'reasonable accommodation' was not coined by those who created the Commission. However, it took on an important new meaning in the notoriously complex and difficult context of Québec society. This new shade of meaning had a Jewish context. Pierre Anctil, who has extensively studied the Jewish community in Québec, utilized the phrase 'accommodement raisonnable' in an op-ed essay in 2006, to characterize the resolution of a dispute between Hasidic Jews in the Montreal suburb of Outremont and the local YMCA over the proximity of windows of the Y's exercise room and a Hasidic synagogue, whose worshippers were uncomfortable viewing women in their exercise garb. Anctil found, however, that: 'ces remarques faites dans la presse avaient été reprises par plusieurs intervenants et généralisées à l'ensemble des personnes appartenant aux communautés récemment immigrées au Québec.'[1]

'Reasonable accommodation' was thus launched on the often troubled seas of the linguistic, ethnic, and cultural identity of Québec. Commission hearings were held in 22 locations throughout Québec in the autumn of 2007, and were widely followed and commented upon in the media in Québec[2] and in the rest of Canada.[3] With the province and the country as a whole watching with rapt attention, the Commission hearings seemed to evoke 'bitter passion and baffled grievance' in numerous presentations.[4] It seemed to many Québecers who appeared before the Commission that immigrants and religious minorities were making excessive societal demands, and this seemed to reinforce negative stereotypes in a French Canadian society that is sensitive to perceived threats to French dominance in the province, debates these issues openly, and deals with ethnic differences in ways that are different from the 'political correctness' practised in much of the rest of North America.[5] The debate that ensued, though, seemed to a number of observers to go beyond previous bounds, and some of them feared that it might portend a possible backlash which could lead to 'serious persecution of minorities, particularly religious minorities.'[6] It certainly led to calls for a crackdown on open displays of non-Christian religions in public spaces.[7] B'nai Brith's 2007 audit of anti-Semitism in Canada drew attention to a surge of anti-Semitic incidents in Québec during the period of the Commission hearings, and attributed the surge to latent feelings of anti-Semitism among Québecers unleashed by the hearings.[8]

A major focus of the Commission's deliberations concerned the place of the Québec Muslim community[9] and other cultural and religious communities such as the Sikhs,[10] whose presence in Québec society has become a prominent issue only in recent years. However, another issue of interest in a significantly large number of submissions to the Commission concerned Judaism and the Jewish community in Québec. Issues raised publicly in and around the Commission with respect to the Jewish community included the Hasidic community, kosher food, visible Jewish symbols such as male head covering [kipa, yarmulke], Jewish schools, and the Jewish character of publicly funded health institutions such as Montreal's Jewish General Hospital. We will now examine how these issues played out in the context of the Commission and its impact on Québec society.

The Conundrums of Contemporary Québec Identity

Political Scientist Garth Stevenson succinctly presents the consensus position which obtains in a large part of Québec society concerning the massive changes in its recent history that are collectively referred to as the Quiet Revolution.

> In the early 1950s, Québec was devoutly Catholic, politically and socially conservative, economically dominated by an Anglophone elite, and seemingly resigned to its provincial status ... By 1976 it was probably the most secular and socially liberal part of North America.[11]

Québec was able to make these changes, while retaining its distinct identity, through shifting its socio-cultural focus from religion to the French language and culture (Weinfeld 2008: 1). Yet precisely in this self-perceived secular and socially liberal province, numerous presentations before the Bouchard-Taylor Commission from September to December of 2007 showed a side of Québec public opinion that was perceived as racist and xenophobic.[12] Thus, another aspect of

Québec society, going quite against its public self-perception, was revealed to a fascinated and sometimes dumbfounded public.[13] Contemporary Québec is also a society in which, as Stevenson further states, 'the legacy of the Quiet Revolution, and the moral and spiritual vacuum that has followed the collapse of clerical power in Québec, are increasingly being questioned.'[14] This questioning has been spurred not least by the rise of a relatively new political party in the province, the Action démocratique du Québec. Its leader, Mario Dumont, has publicly put forward positions designed to protect Québec's 'common values and assert our collective personality.'[15] These positions achieved great resonance among French Québecers, who, in the 2007 provincial election, propelled Dumont's party to official opposition status and are widely cited as one of the main political factors in the Liberal government of Québec's creation of the Bouchard-Taylor Commission.[16]

Québec society's reaction to the perceived crisis of 'reasonable accommodation' is perhaps captured by Québec politician and academic Louise Beaudoin, who attributed Québec's societal malaise that resulted in Bouchard-Taylor in the following way: 'Peut-être que cette réaction a été provoquée par la demande formulée par d'autres communautés de réintroduire la religion dans l'espace publique.'[17]

An example of the sort of issue meant by Beaudoin, and one certainly very much on the minds of the public, was equality of the sexes, which was perceived by many as being in danger from a resurgent religion in the public space on the part of *'d'autres communautés.'* Thus the Québec Council on the Status of Women, a group appointed to advise the Québec government on women's issues, advocated requiring 'public employees to remove visible religious signs when on the job.'[18] Québec Premier Jean Charest, deciding not to wait on this issue until the Commission's report, responded by promising to amend the Québec Charter of Human Rights to give equality of the sexes priority over other rights protected in the Charter.[19]

Who these 'other communities' might be was a rather open secret. These concerns were largely aimed at the public presence of the rapidly expanding Muslim community of Québec.[20] However, Québec's public discourse and many submissions to the Commission concerned the long-established Jewish community in the province, most particularly Orthodox and Hasidic Jews, whose alleged preferential treatment had aroused considerable negative coverage in the French-language media of Québec.[21]

Bouchard-Taylor and the Jews

Jews have lived in Québec since the eighteenth century. They have enjoyed a large communal presence, particularly in Montreal, since the turn of the twentieth century (Tulchinsky 1992, 1998; Robinson and Butofsky 1995). Despite this long presence, the long-standing identification of the majority of the Jewish community with the province's anglophone minority means that the Québec Jewish community remains largely isolated from, and mysterious to, the surrounding francophone milieu in Québec (Weinfeld 2008: 2, 5). It is little wonder, therefore, that Jews, though hardly newcomers to Québec, became quickly associated with Muslims with respect to the public discourse surrounding the Commission. Thus in a recent poll a large minority of francophone Québecers (41 per cent) responded positively to the statement 'The Jews want to impose their customs and traditions on others,' while only 31 per cent said yes to the proposition 'Jews want to participate fully in society.'[22]

While it is arguable that most Jews (and Muslims) are indeed well integrated into Québec society, the focus of the testimony before the Commission revolved around those areas in which Jews became a visible minority to many Québecers and were alleged to have made concrete (and excessive) demands for accommodation in Québec. Kosher food, which serves to differentiate observant Jews from the food ways of their fellow citizens, became an issue. Thus some presenters to the Commission, echoing the claims of American white supremacist organizations,[23] charged that the Jewish community was forcing food companies to pay for kashrut certification, change their formulas, and raise their prices in order to obtain kosher certification, thus affecting all Québecers, who had to pay higher prices for their food.[24]

There were expressions of opposition to government funding for Jewish day schools, which in 2005 had been a divisive issue in Québec politics when the Liberal minister of education for Québec moved to increase the level of government subsidies for the Jewish school system and was forced to back down under tremendous public pressure directed against 'the powerful Jewish lobby,' which was alleged to have obtained this subsidy as a quid pro quo for Jewish political and financial support for the Liberal Party of Québec.[25] Significantly, government support for Jewish (and other) faith-based schools in Québec echoed another *cause célèbre* in Québec educational politics, the creation of a new curriculum dealing with world religions to replace an older curriculum in Christianity and moral education.[26]

The Hasidic community, the epitome of visible Judaism in Québec and the focus of considerable tension in the Montreal suburb of Outremont (Schnoor 2002), was described by several presenters as a major problem. In the hearing held in the city of St. Jerome, several presentations focused on tensions between French Canadian residents of the Laurentians and an 'ever growing number' of Hasidim making 'unreasonable' demands.[27] The previously discussed issue of the Hasidic synagogue and the Montreal YWCA was broached.[28] One presenter, Pierre Lacerte, charged that the Hasidim are 'powerful, stubborn and pugnacious,' bearing 'special privileges.'[29] Others described them as 'money-driven profiteers of the immigration system, determined to force their archaic ways on the Québec majority with their kosher foods, large families, loud prayers, and separate lives.'[30]

Public perceptions of special privileges for Jews made an issue of whether hospitals like the Jewish General Hospital of Montreal, with its kosher cafeterias and a Hebrew motto on its seal, belonged in Québec.[31] An incident during which a medical clinic [CLSC] saw an Orthodox Jew on a Friday afternoon before his turn in order to accommodate his Sabbath observance was also broached.[32]

Finally, the place of religious symbolism in a secular society became one of the foci of the debate, echoing the aforementioned statement of the Québec Council on the Status of Women advising the government 'to force public employees to remove visible religious signs when they are on the job,' including specifically 'Jewish yarmulkes.'[33]

The official response of the Jewish community of Québec to the widespread nature of the controversy was determinedly low-key. The establishment of the Montreal Jewish community, Federation/CJA, chose not to formally present a public statement to the Commission. It rather chose to be represented through a brief presented by the Canadian Jewish Congress, Québec Region, part of whose mandate is intercommunity relations.[34] The president of Montreal's Federation/CJA, Marc Gold, stated that his organization was determined 'not to respond publicly to every comment made ... believing it would not serve the best interests of the community.'[35] The brief presented by the Canadian Jewish Congress (CJC) was in large part an attempt to answer charges that had been raised against Jews and Judaism during the hearings, such as the alleged prevalence of Jewish 'wealth and influence'[36] and the higher cost of kosher food. As well, the brief opposed the precedence of gender equality over religious freedom and supported the right of workers in public institutions to wear religious symbols. The main spokesman for the CJC, and hence for the community, Dr Victor Goldbloom, tried his best to emphasize the positive and to underline the community of values shared by the Jewish community and Québec as a whole. As he stated, 'The Québec Jewish community ... shares Québec values and experiences, an overall accommodation which is more than reasonable.'[37] The brief presented to the Commission by the Jewish General Hospital likewise accentuated the positive and presented a picture of the hospital that is captured in the title of the brief, 'Care For All.' It presented itself as an institution that has practiced reasonable accommodation for decades, and emphasized that the concept 'is a sound one, as long as it is sensibly applied, fairly administered, and able to balance the rights and needs of the minority with those of the majority.'[38] Allegations against the hospital were passed over in silence.

B'nai Brith Canada, Québec Region, was the third major Jewish organization to submit a brief to the Commission. It is known for its activist response to incidents and expressions of anti-Semitism. Its response was, predictably, somewhat less moderated than that of the CJC. The nature of B'nai Brith's submission, like that of the Jewish General Hospital, is captured in its title, 'Accommodation and Differences: Seeking Common Ground: Québecers Speak Out.' The brief noted that:

> Misunderstandings about the concept of Reasonable Accommodation have served to fuel this debate, dividing Québec society along minority/religious group lines, thus creating a climate of animosity and mistrust towards new immigrants, as well as existing cultural/religious communities ... We are concerned that there is mounting tension in the province, contributing to an increased climate of hostility ...[39]

This brief is notable in that it alone criticized the Québec government's lack of action 'in the removal of barriers to the employment of cultural minorities in the public and quasi-public sector.'[40]

Reaction by individual members of the Montreal Jewish community, unlike the official communal response, tended to emphasize the shock and distress afforded by the xenophobic character of some of the presentations.[41] Thus McGill professor Gil Troy criticized the Commission's 'giving the narrow-minded a platform for broadcasting their virus – and feeling validated by the applause they received ... to become local heroes and to have their virus taken seriously.' In his view, 'The commission's greatest failure stems from the silence we have heard in reacting to the bigots ... the uncomfortable silences and awkward half-hearted defenses amid the bigotry' (Weinfeld 2008: 7). Others, like the Orthodox Rabbi Chaim Steinmetz, sought to discern the larger issues in play, and stated: 'At issue is not head coverings or the gender of driving-test examiners, but the very sense of cooperation and trust required in a functioning society.'[42]

Indeed, B'nai B'rith's League for Human Rights, in its 2006 audit of anti-Semitic incidents, commented:

> Public reaction to reports of the special needs of religious minorities has become increasingly vocal and, at times, openly hostile ... Societal tensions around the issue of 'reasonable accommodation' are not merely a reaction to the latest news story but reflect a growing upsurge in the level of prejudice that lies just beneath the surface of society, waiting to erupt.[43]

Towards a Historical Contextualization

The debate surrounding the issue of reasonable accommodation in Québec has not ceased by any means. The Commission officially released its report at the end of May 2008,[44] in which it recommended a number of measures having a potential impact on the Jewish community. Most particularly, it recommended that government employees who 'embody the state,' such as judges and police officers, should not be allowed to wear religious symbols such as a *kipot*, while other public employees, such as physicians, could be allowed to wear them. The report found that the Québec Jewish community is diverse and increasingly French-speaking, and stated that 'it is in Québec society's interests to get to know the Jewish community better.' Its investigation of numerous media reports of abuse of reasonable accommodation found that most of them contained 'striking distortions' or incomplete information. It particularly stated that the accusation that making food kosher raised the price of food products for non-Jewish consumers is greatly exaggerated and that any cost increase to the consumer is 'very minimal.' It found that anti-Semitism should be combated by extraordinary measures, but rejected accusations that the Commission's hearings had themselves contributed to anti-Jewish prejudice.[45]

Inevitably, the release of the report has spurred considerable public comment within Québec society and in Canada as a whole. Initial reaction from the Montreal Jewish community was as low-key as its input during the Commission's hearings. Victor Goldbloom, the point man of the Canadian Jewish Congress, Québec Region, immediately congratulated Bouchard and Taylor on the job they had done, and underlined the Québec Jewish community's historical roots and its commitment to the French language, gender equality, and the values of the Québec Charter of Human Rights and Freedoms.[46] Somewhat later, Goldbloom noted his disagreement with the Commission's recommendation that prominent public servants like judges not be allowed to wear religious symbols, deeming such a measure an infringement of religious freedom and liable to bar Orthodox Jews from holding such positions. While implicitly criticizing the Commission's handling of some anti-Semitic comments at its hearings, particularly at first, he emphasized that 'the co-chairs are absolutely decent people, and in no way can they be considered to have condoned any of these negative things.' B'nai Brith criticized the Commission's recommendations as being 'overly simplistic and naïve.' Finally, Alex Werzberger, a spokesman for Montreal's Hasidic community, welcomed the report, and hopefully opined that it would help to 'improve the atmosphere.'[47]

More important for our considerations, however, is the fact that the current debate needs to be seen against the broader historical context of the often troubled confrontation of French Canadians and Jews in the twentieth century.[48] As Weinfeld has pointed out, 'French Québec has not come to a full societal resolution of its attitude toward the Jews ... during the 1930s and 1940s' (Weinfeld 2008: 7). In this historical context some specific issues in dispute with respect to Jews in Québec have indeed changed. One hundred years ago, for instance, issues concerning kosher food were almost exclusively internal to the Jewish community and involved kosher meat almost exclusively (Robinson 2007). It is worth noting in this context that Québec in the 1920s and 1930s never generated a significant, let alone successful, campaign to ban the kosher slaughter of animals, such as occurred in such countries as Germany, Switzerland, Poland, and Norway.[49] The current allegations against the added price to consumers of kosher certification have nothing to do with kosher meat, which is a commodity that does not affect non-Jewish consumers. They are rather a reflection of the ubiquity of kosher-certified food products in contemporary North American supermarkets, and the perceived demand for kosher certification on the part of consumers who wish to purchase kosher products for reasons that transcend those of kashrut-observant Jews.[50]

Another important change involves the nature of the Jewish 'irritant' in French Canadian society. In the early twentieth century, for instance, Jews as such were 'visible' to the French Canadian community, and the presence of Jews in the Laurentians was deemed objectionable (Tulchinsky 1998). By the early twenty-first century, the presence of Montreal Jews and their summer homes in the Laurentians had become fairly widespread and non-controversial. Open conflict and controversy in the Laurentians with respect to Jews now seems mostly confined to the Hasidic community. The situation has evolved in this way at least partially because Hasidim have become the symbolic 'visible' Jews in Québec society, and male Hasidic garb has been used, in editorial cartoons and elsewhere, as media shorthand for 'Jew.' Moreover, the Hasidim, who tend to live in close proximity to one another, are visible to the rest of society in a way that most other Jews are not (even though most Jews in Québec, and not merely Hasidim, also tend to live in 'Jewish' neighbourhoods) (Weinfeld 2008). It is clear that this visible Hasidic presence in Québec society is a fairly recent phenomenon. Despite evidence of a Hasidic presence in Canada early in the twentieth century (Lapidus 2004), the historical memory of the current Hasidic community in Québec does not extend beyond the 1940s, and a demographically significant Hasidic community appeared in the public view of Québec more or less simultaneously with other immigrant communities from Asia, Africa, and other places. This goes a considerable way towards explaining the prominence of Jews in a context in which the focus was largely on communities recently established in Québec.

A further issue of note in this survey is that in the early twentieth century, French Canadians considered themselves economically subordinated to 'the English,' and expressed their resentment of this situation in campaigns like '*achat chez nous*,' which impacted upon the Québec Jewish community of the era. In the early twenty-first century, it is clear that the Quiet Revolution has achieved many of its economic goals and has changed both perceptions and facts concerning French Canadian economic power. Nonetheless, the fact that Jews came under criticism at the Bouchard-Taylor Commission for their economic power[51] indicates that this may be an area in which '*plus ça change, plus c'est la même chose.*'

Whatever has changed, it seems that the place of Jews as 'others' to most French Canadians has not. The key difference, in the context of the early twenty-first century, is that in the early twentieth century the Jewish community was the sole significant non-Christian, non-Aboriginal group in Québec. It has now been joined by Muslims, Hindus, Sikhs, and a host of others. Québec society, like many societies, is torn between inclinations towards global inclusivity and ethnic exclusivism. The debate that launched the Commission came about because, as Henry Aubin, a Quebec journalist for the *Gazette*, points out, in contemporary Québec '[o]vert ethnic nationalism is becoming respectable after a long hibernation.'[52] Whether this nationalism will go back into hibernation or remain a present and powerful force within Québec society will depend to some extent on how that society receives and accepts the Bouchard-Taylor Commission's report, which, in the advanced reporting, was characterized as 'a road map for modern Québec to better integrate religious and immigrant minorities.'[53]

4 'Qui est nous?' Some Answers from the Bouchard-Taylor Commission's Archive

BINA TOLEDO FREIWALD

Preliminaries

> The present debate interpellates me personally as regards our being as a collectivity.
> — André Godin (2007: 2)[1]

'Qui est nous?' (literally, 'Who is we?') is the question that François Parenteau's documentary *Qui est nous?* (first aired on Telé-Québec 21 February 2002) poses to its 11 subjects, all identified as Québecers who have come from elsewhere (other cultures), that is, who cannot claim French Canadian ancestry. The film invites them to reflect on their sense of identity and belonging in Québec, and in many ways is an emblematic precursor to the province-wide exercise in collective soul-searching that journalists Jeff Heinrich and Valérie Dufour (2008) have dubbed 'Circus Québécus.'

The primary focus of this chapter is the very large textual archive generated by the 2007 Consultation Commission on Accommodation Practices Related to Cultural Differences (hereafter the Bouchard-Taylor Commission), chaired by Gérard Bouchard and Charles Taylor. My principal interest is in the written briefs ('mémoires') submitted by individuals from across the province in response to the commissioners' invitation to citizens – in a Consultation Document entitled *Accommodation and Differences: Seeking Common Ground: Québecers Speak Out* – to make themselves heard on the subject of 'the nature and source of the conflict that is dividing Québec society in order to imagine the means of reconciliation' (Bouchard and Taylor 2007b: vi).

Bouchard and Taylor made it clear in the opening section of the Consultation Document that the focus of their commission would not be on legalistic matters pertaining to accommodation practices (the initial impetus for the creation of the Commission), but rather on the broader and fraught issue of 'Québec identity,' of which they saw the reasonable accommodation debate to be a symptom (v). From the outset, then, the Commission foreclosed on a range of other possible approaches to the issue of social justice and integration, approaches that individuals and organizations would nonetheless try to bring to the table through their oral and written presentations regarding, for example, the sources of economic disadvantage, the workings of ethnic/racial discrimination, and the legacy of colonialism in the treatment of First Nations.[2] Both Parenteau's (2002) documentary and the Bouchard-Taylor Commission's mandate accord paramount importance to the issue of collective identity, understood as rooted in one's culture of origin, and both are premised on an acceptance of the hegemony of the majority group, in relation to whom all others are defined by the somewhat threatening demands they make: to be accommodated, to be granted entry into the charmed circle of belonging.

On another level, Parenteau's grammatically awkward but suggestive title, by conjoining the singular with the plural, serves as an important double reminder as we broach the issue of collective identity at the centre of the documentary and the Commission. First, it reminds us that there is no 'we' without an 'I.' In trying to settle the question of identity in Québec, both Parenteau's documentary and the Commission have no other choice but to resort to individual articulations of collective identity, confirming what theorists of nationalism have long recognized: namely, that national and other collective identifications are always 'imagined' (Anderson 1991: 6), and thus are inescapably 'mediated through the self' (Cohen 2000: 146). The referent of a collective identity cannot be a given, it has to be continuously constructed by individual acts of self-fashioning. Thus the arena of personal narratives, which includes the testimonies featured in Parenteau's documentary and the individual briefs presented to the Bouchard-Taylor Commission, constitutes a privileged site of study, allowing us to examine up-close the manner in which individual subjects imagine their collectivity.

The flip side of the same coin is that while there is no 'we' without an 'I,' there is also no 'I' without a 'we'; as social psychologist George Mead (1936: 375) put it, 'the human self arises through its ability to take the attitude of the group to which he belongs.' In this respect, too, personal narratives provide us with a unique opportunity to explore both how individual subjects come to construct their identity out of the social scripts made available to them by the groups within which they are embedded, and how these subjects' existential and affective investment in a sense of belonging to these groups provide them with the very terms out of which selfhood can be fashioned. Individual identity, as sociologists and psychologists concur, emerges in relation to an other within a grid of collective identifications (familial, gendered, ethnic, religious, national, etc.) that bring the subject into being through what Althusser (1971: 163) calls 'interpellation or hailing.'

Since there is no 'I' without a 'we,' the need to belong has been characterized as 'a fundamental human motivation,' seen by social psychologists as one of the core human needs (positioned between the basic physiological and safety needs and the higher-level esteem and self-actualization needs), and by neuropsychologists as an innate need mediated by opioid peptides, and thus literally addictive (Franken 1998: 327–33). An addictive yet fundamental driving force, belonging is a socially and ideologically fraught pursuit. It is a condition beset by anxiety, since it is ultimately a privilege only the collectivity can grant (by agreeing that you are one of us), and it rests on a paradoxical ideological proposition: based on a principle of inclusion, it is premised on the exercise of its opposite, exclusion. Social psychologists have offered the following explanation linking individuals' need for a sense of collective belonging to the inevitability of intergroup exclusionary dynamics, hostility, and conflict: 'intergroup conflict is central to one's sense of self. In an effort to feel good about one's self, it is important for people to feel good about the groups to which they belong, and one means for achieving this is to see one's own groups as better than out-groups' (Park and Judd 2005: 110).

The challenge, then, for humans as social animals, has been to imagine a model of self/other co-existence that would encourage intergroup harmony while recognizing and valuing the distinctions that make up the shared social sphere. This challenge becomes particularly acute in the case of liberal democracies characterized by diverse populations, such as Canada and Québec, and the Bouchard-Taylor Commission's archive allows us to examine the manner in which this tension between 'recognizing and valuing group identities, and retaining a sense of shared commonalities' (Park and Judd 2005: 125) is articulated in both the official discourse and in individual citizens' responses to it.

The Commissioners' Mission (Impossible?): Seeking Common Ground

> [interculturalism] seeks to combine on an equal footing two elements that are *a priori* hard to reconcile, i.e. respect for diversity and the imperatives of collective integration.
> — Bouchard and Taylor (2007b: 19)

In *The Unfinished Canadian: The People We Are*, Andrew Cohen (2007) suggests that Canada, like many other countries today, is profoundly preoccupied with the question of collective identity: 'Who are we? Where do we belong?' (7). Cohen concludes with the prediction that 'the threats to Canada will come from immigration and decentralization,' since 'Much as they will enrich Canada, immigrants will challenge it. The strains of multiculturalism are already emerging' (256). While Cohen tries to dissociate the terms of Canadian identity from what he describes as Québec's ethnic nationalism, and bemoans Parliament's resolution in 2006 to recognize *les Québécois* as a nation, his own perception of immigration and pluralism as identitarian threats is not much different from sentiments expressed in many of the briefs submitted to the Bouchard-Taylor Commission. The Commission's hearings and the briefs from individuals and organizations submitted to it show a citizenry in the throes of an existential-identitarian dilemma which manifests itself symptomatically in expressions of anxiety about the Other. This dilemma currently occupies centre stage in Québec, but it resonates with many other liberal democracies around the world.

In Québec, Elspeth Probyn (1996) has observed, 'identity is an institutional project' and the 'constant appeals to belong' are impossible to avoid (67).[3] In his critical examination of the main identity narratives in Québec since the 1950s, Jocelyn Maclure (2003) concludes that the theme underlying the heated debates over 'the question of identity' has been 'the challenge of pluralism' (xi–xii). To identify one aspect of this existential drama, which I see as a focal point in both the commissioner's Consultation Document and many of the briefs submitted to the Commission, I draw on Ronald Beiner's (2003) analysis in *Liberalism, Nationalism, Citizenship: Essays on the Problem of Political Community*. Using case studies that include Québec, Canada, and Israel, Beiner argues that one of the greatest challenges facing liberal democracies today, given their appeal to universalizing principles of social cohesion, is articulating the grounds for an allegiance to any given political community. In such a context, Beiner asks what might constitute satisfactory answers to questions such as, 'Why commit one's political allegiance to *this* political community rather than *that* political community? What are the *bounds* of political community, and on what basis do citizens commit themselves emotionally and existentially (as actually defining their own identity) to some specific, identifiable community of fellow citizens?' (166). The problem is further exacerbated, since not only is it likely that there would be competing conceptions of citizenship circulating within a given society, but each of the main available conceptions also leaves some crucial issues unresolved. The *'liberal conception of citizenship'* (167) with its emphasis on the rule of law and protection of universal human rights, and the *'welfarist conception of citizenship'* in which the allegiance is to a state defined by the social benefits it offers (167), both fail to provide what Beiner calls a robust experience of identity; within these models, what would keep a citizen from turning to another state offering similar rights and benefits? The *'pluralist conception of identity'* (167), for its part, risks encouraging multiple group identities that could eventually trump allegiance to the state. Finally, *'nationalism,'* with its specific ethnolinguistic, cultural, or religious referents does elicit a robust identitarian attachment, but at the price of lessening a commitment to 'universal humanity' (168).

Beiner (2003) expresses skepticism regarding the prospects of an easy reconciliation between nationalism, which he views as by definition having an ethnic referent, and liberalism, since in a world where most states are multi-ethnic or multinational, 'any robust appeal to 'the nation' ... will make it very difficult to sustain the idea of equality of all citizens' (203). Yet it is precisely with an appeal to imagine such a reconciliation between nationalism and liberalism that Bouchard and Taylor invited Québecers, in the fall of 2007, to participate in our own version of a truth and reconciliation process, launching the process with the Consultation Document, *Accommodation And Differences: Seeking Common Ground: Québecers Speak Out*. The Consultation Document invited Québecers to speak out, but through the power of 'constitutive rhetoric' (Charland 1987: 134) it also told Québecers who they are – thus inviting a particular kind of response from them – by naming or interpellating the different constituencies that make up the collectivity. Clearly informed by contemporary theorizations of the liberal democratic state, the Consultation Document sets not only the stage but also the terms for the debate it invites. And these terms, I would suggest, are haunted by the spectre of the 'nation,' which, as Beiner (2003) argues, makes it difficult to sustain the idea of equality of all citizens.

The Consultation Document clearly states that the commissioners understand their task to go beyond the symptomatic concerns about reasonable accommodation, in order to address the 'more basic problem concerning the socio-cultural integration model that has prevailed in Québec since the 1970s and the issue of "Québec identity"' (Bouchard and Taylor 2007b: v). The document provides a template of five available models of community: assimilation, the mixing of cultures, multi-ethnicity, the civic nation, and interculturalism. The commissioners openly declare their endorsement of Québec's model of interculturalism, which aims 'to combine on an equal footing two elements that are *a priori* hard to reconcile, i.e. respect for diversity and the imperatives of collective integration' (19). It becomes apparent from the rhetoric and logic of the document that diversity and integration are hard to reconcile, more specifically in the case of Québec because not all of the elements that make up its diverse citizenry are qualitatively equal. In the broader identitarian map that Bouchard and Taylor draw up in the Consultation Document, only two groups are granted the privileged status of 'nation' or a 'people': 'Québecers of French-Canadian origin ... a founding people established for four centuries in this territory,' and the 'aboriginal peoples' (4). The other groups that populate Québec and the rest of Canada are of a different kind: language is the sole marker used to designate the 'English-speaking minority' in Québec (3) as well as the broader entity, 'English-speaking Canada' (5): the rest come under the rubric of 'ethnic minorities' (4) or 'cultural communities' (14). It becomes evident from the Document's rhetoric that nation or peoplehood trump both language and ethnicity. A nation, unlike other types of groups, is justified in its anxiety over 'survival' (19), and in its struggle to safeguard the national 'values and institutions ... its heritage' (9).

Distinguishing Québec's interculturalism model from Canadian multiculturalism, Bouchard and Taylor (2007b) present the latter as originally stemming from the demands of ethnic minorities from Western Canada seeking recognition of their identity, but immediately add that these groups were 'among the best integrated' (19). This emphasis on integration and the absence in the document of any acknowledgment of the question of Canadian identity suggest that, for the commissioners, multiculturalism is a model for a citizenry that does not partake of a specifically national character and thus has a much weaker investment in particularistic identities. Tellingly, the Consultation Document often rhetorically confuses or conflates two current but rather conflicting meanings of 'nation': 'nation' in the sense of a distinct people characterized by common descent and an accrued shared history that includes a common language and culture; and 'nation' in the inclusive sense of the citizenry of a country or a state (which might be multinational). Such confusion or conflation occurs, for example, in the statement, 'The relationship between the aboriginal peoples and Québec is a nation-to-nation relationship' (4) where 'nation,' in referring to 'the aboriginal peoples,' clearly means peoplehood by descent; whereas 'nation,' in referring to 'Québec,' seems to refer to the political (provincial) entity comprising citizens of diverse descents. Such slippages allow the commissioners to avoid addressing the crucial question regarding the relation – in the Québec context – between 'nation' as it figures in statements that align Québec with other 'Western nations' that are similarly pluralistic (nation as country/state), and 'nation' understood in the narrower sense of a distinct people, as articulated in a tenet of interculturalism stipulating that minority groups can preserve elements of their culture on the condition that they combine them with the foundational elements of the majority/national culture, 'borrow[ing] from its basic values and customs, adopt[ing] the French language, and shar[ing] the national heritage and the Québec identity' (21).

In *Shall We Dance? A Patriotic Politics for Canada*, Charles Blattberg (2003) reflects on precisely such a conflation of the concepts of citizenry and nation. He distinguishes between six kinds of community – '*civil associations, ethnicities, religions, regions, nations, and citizenries*' (59) – and cautions against the tendency to conflate the last two. Blattberg contends that only the concept of 'shared citizenry' – premised on conversation and dialogue in which all the parts that make up the whole work together towards the realization of the 'single public common good that they all share' (79) – can offer a model for embracing a country's diversity, including its multinational or multi-ethnic character. The common good around which a citizenry coalesces, he argues, is very different from the common good that constitutes the national community. When the predominant model is that of the nation, which appears to be the case with interculturalism, integration becomes problematic, since the nationalist's interests are oriented differently, privileging the identitarian demands of a particularistic constituency: 'First, there is the nationalist's concern for his or her nation's cultural heritage ... Second, the nationalist affirms a special attachment to a particular piece of land ... And third, nationalists lay claim to a sense that their nation cannot be considered free unless it receives a particular form of recognition from the state(s) under whose jurisdiction it lives' (63).

'Like other Western nations,' Bouchard and Taylor (2007b) write in the Consultation Document, 'Québec must find a way to draw together different cultures sharing the same space and that rely on the same institutions' (vii). However, according to the terms of the interculturalism model that they endorse, the space that is Québec is not inhabited by different cultures but rather by a nation and its others (the document acknowledges the existence of the First Nations but completely leaves them out of the discussion, a decision a number of First Nations participants find objectionable). Thus, from the outset the Consultation Document attempts to reconcile what Beiner and Blattberg identify as competing models, seeking to find a common ground between nationalism and a hybrid liberal/welfarist/pluralist citizenship model. Throughout the Consultation Document and then the final report that was released in May 2008, we witness the conceptual and rhetorical strains of this attempted reconciliation. On the one hand, there are expressions of distress on behalf of a national community. Bouchard and Taylor write in the Consultation Document: 'Many nations are today facing the reaction of established identities that are being destabilized by tenacious diversity.' This is then immediately followed up by an insistence on the moral imperative of pluralism: 'Such nations must also shape a pluralistic awareness that gradually took root in the second half of the 20th century' (vi). In their final report, *Building the Future, a Time for Reconciliation* (2008), trying to present a vision that is both hopeful and pragmatic, the commissioners can often do no better than offer a string of rhetorical equivocations yoking together conflicting demands. What interculturalism aims for, they write, is: 'reconciling the imperatives of pluralism stemming from the growing diversification of our society and the necessary integration of a small nation that constitutes a cultural minority in North America' (93). The imperative, they repeat, is, 'integration through pluralism,' to 'promote an identity, a culture and a memory without creating either exclusion or division' (94). This begs the question of whose memory, culture, and identity are to be promoted, and the answer is again to be found in the strained rhetorical turns: '"the others" are consistently lumped together as the anonymous "growing diversity," while the majority is awarded the identitarian badge of honor of recognition as a nation, further legitimated in its identitarian mission by being characterized as a vulnerable small minority nation "mistreated by history"' (94).

In a section of their final report entitled 'Looking to the Future,' Bouchard and Taylor (2008) put forward 'The edification of a common identity' (88) as an arch imperative, but again that vision consists of what are arguably elements from conflicting models of community. On the one hand, the identity they call for has elements from what Beiner (2003) would call 'civicism' (205), a model of political community that is neither national nor transnational, where the binding 'markers of identity are relevant for *every member of the civic community*' (203). Bouchard and Taylor (2008) speak of the development of 'citizen culture, i.e., all Québecers must recognize themselves in it and achieve self-fulfillment through it' (88), an evolving culture characterized by shared values such as gender equality, pluralism, and secularism, where a sense of belonging is developed through civic institutions. But their model also includes the very elements that would inhibit such developments, as their writing keeps circling back to the core tenets of a nationalist discourse. One has to be mindful, they write, that 'French-speaking Québec is a minority culture and needs a strong identity to allay its anxieties and behave like a serene majority' (75); thus, all of the above has to be done 'without harming the French-Canadian heritage' (89). Perhaps, not surprisingly, the report's grand finale, a proposed amalgam of eight avenues for the edification of a common Québec identity, confirms Beiner's (2003) characterization of Taylor's earlier writings on this subject as 'simultaneously liberal, civicist, nationalist, and multiculturalist' (210).

Québecers Speak Out: An Identitarian Drama Unfolds

> The problem [literally, the drama] lies in the fact that the Canadian and Québec Charters, for all practical purposes, only recognize individual rights. This is an error to correct ... Our collective rights [as First Nations] therefore have to be taken into consideration.
> — Max Gros-Louis (2003: 3)[4]

As one reads through the hundreds of briefs presented to the Bouchard-Taylor Commission by individuals and organizations from across the province, it becomes apparent that the commissioners' invitation to reflect on the question of collective identity did strike a chord among the citizenry. Journalists Jeff Heinrich and Valérie Dufour (2008), who followed the Commission and wrote about it in *Circus Québécus: Sous le chapiteau de la commission Bouchard-Taylor*, report that close to 3,500 people attended the public forums, and many of those who spoke came prepared with carefully composed texts (180). There are a total of 843 briefs posted on the Commission's site, of which 601, or 71 per cent, are by individuals, and the rest from organized groups.

The desire to identify and claim a plural 'we' within which the 'I' could belong is a common theme that runs through the briefs, evident from across the range of ethnic self-identifications. André Godin (2007), resident of Sherbrooke, writes: 'Every human being normally searches for an answer to this question: Who am I in the surrounding collectivity? The collectivity, too, asks itself the same question: Who are we as a Québécois collectivity?' (3).[5] In his brief, Godin elaborates on what he sees as a set of values that characterizes Québec society, but as in many of the briefs by self-identified *de souche*, or old-stock Québécois, this set of civic values is ultimately an *added value*, added on to something expressed as more primary yet often left unspecified: the 'heritage' of Québec society, 'its culture ... its traditions.'[6] Godin writes: 'This heritage *also consists* of founding values we consider non-negotiable, such as equality among people regardless of race, religion, or ethnicity; democracy; and freedom of expression and religion' (8; emphasis added).[7] In many such briefs, the writer's desire to foreground a universalistic civic character to the Québécois collectivity comes up against a profound attachment to the particularistic identity of a people and the nation. The predicament is bluntly articulated in Jean-Francois Lisée's (2007) brief entitled, 'For a new equilibrium between all of "Us" Québécois.'[8] The common denominators of a civic democracy – equality, rights, and freedoms – are of course important, Lisée concedes, but they cannot come at the expense of an affirmation of the majority's identitarian distinctiveness, without which respect for both self and other would be lost: 'We must start by restoring the majoritarian reference points. What are they? Democracy, gender equality, charter of rights, freedom of religion? Fine, that's understood! We've just chimed out the common denominator of all democratic societies. No. I speak of the Québécois difference. In bold strokes: Québec exists because its majority has experienced a singular history, speaks French and carries a religious tradition. To evacuate them, to devalue them, could only lead to losing one's self-esteem and, in the long run, hating the other' (3).[9]

In the broader identitarian landscape that emerges from the briefs, the position of Jean-Francois Lisée and many other self-identified old-stock

Québécois finds its mirror image in presentations to the commissions by First Nations individuals and groups. The words of Max 'One-Onti' Gros-Louis, Grand Chief of the Huron-Wendat Nation, cited in the epigraph to this section, echo Lisée's argument that an overemphasis on shared liberal democratic values risks putting into jeopardy the difference that constitutes the national collectivity. Gros-Louis (2007) bemoans the fact that the commissioners have decided not to include the 'nation-to-nation' relationship between Québec and the First Nations as part of their mandate – pointing out that the reality on the ground falls far short of this ideal model – and further suggests that the First Nations have a valuable lesson to teach nationalist Québecers. He cautions: 'we are the best example of what could happen to you if you allow yourselves to become like us, a disempowered minority at the mercy of others who would impose their own way of being on you' (5).[10]

As the language of many briefs by self-identified old-stock Québécois suggests, the attachment to the 'Québécois difference' of which Lisée speaks is a properly national sentiment, and draws on a founding trope of the discourse of peoplehood: blood descent. André Godin (2007) reminds us that one's first sense of identity is acquired through the family, which passes on a heritage that includes 'language, religion and a social culture' (4).[11] One could add that what the family also instills in the child, before any critical faculty has developed, is the model of 'blood loyalty,' of blood belonging (Ignatieff 1993: 9), arguably an affectively compelling model of collective identification and one that nationalism embraces in its literal and figurative appeal to kinship. Symptomatic of this attachment to a kinship model of collective identity are the biblical-style recitations of genealogy in briefs by self-identified old-stock Québécois. Saguenay resident Marcien Bisson (2007) explains his interest in the mandate of the Commission and the question of Québec identity by invoking his familial-cum-national history, and thus his claim to this place: 'I belong to the founding people of this country. About 800 ancestors on my father's side and about as many on my mother's. Eleven generations of Bisson, Tardif, Pinard, Bourassa, Fréchette ... etc.' (3).[12] Alain C. Paiement (2007), resident of Gatineau, opens his brief with his own family tree, dating back to his ancestor Jacques Archambault, who in 1658 dug the first well in Montréal: 'You can call me an old-stock Québécois. According to my genealogical notes, my ancestors would have arrived early during the period of the French Regime. At the Pointe-à-Callière Museum, in Montréal, one can read, inscribed on a stone, that that's the place where a certain Jacques Archambault would have dug, in 1658, following the orders of the governor, the first well in Montréal. That Archambault is the ancestor of all the Archambaults. I am one of them' (1).[13]

In this 'I am one of them' lies the particularly powerful appeal of what Beiner (2003) describes as the robust experience of national identity: it allows one to affirm one's being and belonging without equivocation, as the recipient of a great gift one is entitled to for simply being born into the fold. If you turn away from this identity, Paiement (2007) warns, and follow the trendy and misguided cosmopolitan intellectuals, you will end up lost and confused; you will end up, Michel Émery (2007) from Montréal concurs, feeling like 'an abused orphan' (4), 'uprooted from a land I always believed mine and that my people are losing to the globalization of diversities' (5).[14] The intercultural model, Paiement and others challenge the commissioners, has been making schizophrenics of Québecers, asking them to combine in equal measure respect for diversity and the imperative of integration, two objectives that are mutually exclusive and thus cancel each other out, leaving Québecers immobilized, confused, doomed to fail as a society. We all know, Paiement (2007) writes, that 'Two equal and opposed forces result in nothing. This is what we live in Québec. It's a recipe that guarantees paralysis, confusion, the rotting of the social climate and terminal failure' (4).[15]

The great gift of belonging that the nation confers thus comes at a price. Since in the discourse of nationhood the nation is defined as requiring autonomy in order to preserve its character as 'bounded in space, continuous in time, and homogeneous within those spatio-temporal boundaries' (Handler 1988: 50), it is, in consequence, perceived as being 'perpetually threatened. To define existence in terms of boundedness and autonomy simultaneously defines the rest of reality as "other" and sets up an adversary relationship: the nation either controls its destiny or is controlled by others' (51). Moreover, the model of the family-as-nation/the nation-as-family breeds a particular kind of anxiety, for any perceived threat to one's sense of collective identity is affectively experienced as a devastating blow to one's very sense of self. Michel Émery (2007) writes: 'as long as I am an orphan, I will have tremendous difficulties integrating the diversities present on the territory, for I struggle to define myself, feel threatened and do not have the tools to live in full harmony ... I am sorry but I won't respond to your expectations; for the time being my preoccupations are directed towards my people and as far as diversities are concerned, it is integration within the Québécois culture and not the other way round' (7–8).[16]

As demonstrated above, the rhetoric of briefs by self-identified old-stock Québécois suggests the centrality of the concept of peoplehood to their sense of collective identity. However, the clear avoidance in the majority of briefs of the terms of ethnic nationalism leaves open the question of how the collectivity is to be characterized in ways that still articulate a distinctiveness not assimilable to a more universal set of values. Thus, while the insistence on nation and 'peoplehood' is the centre around which many of these briefs circle, filling this centre with content remains a task for each writer to perform. As Richard Handler (1988) observes regarding nationalist discourses in general, 'The existence of a national entity is a primary assumption of nationalist ideology ... but the content of national being is the subject of continual negotiation and dispute' (51).

The French language is an element of the collective identity that is cited by all, but perhaps because of its greater inclusivity (it characterizes many other national cultures), it does not appear to carry the same affective weight as the attachment to the majoritarian religion and its traditions. Interestingly, religion and the religious heritage as identity markers are invoked by writers from the full range of constituencies represented by the briefs, from self-defined old-stock Québécois, both religious and secular, to immigrants of various faiths. Serge Charpentier (2007) of Montréal, who identifies himself as an old-stock Québécois of the Catholic faith, offers his opinion that while everybody acknowledges that the Québécois are a people – the very existence of this Commission, he argues, is a sign of this recognition since only a people would preoccupy itself with the question of how to receive members of other nations[17] – at present that identity is undermined by the disappearance of its foundational religious character: '[W]e have an identity problem as a result of the fact that we have lost one of our foundations. Religion is no longer there' (2).[18] Gisèle Denoncourt (2007), resident of Drummondville, entitles her brief, 'To accommodate, certainly. But holà, let's preserve our common values!' She identifies the common values of her majoritarian culture, which she considers a 'very welcoming and accommodating nation' (3),[19] offering a list she suggests should be communicated to all immigrants, but also to some Québecers in need of enlightenment, and which includes the French language and the familiar liberal democratic principles of gender equality and 'the secular character of the public sphere.' This last value, however, she immediately qualifies with this parenthetical note: '(but not completely, we should not deny our history, our heritage)' (3).[20]

The fear of losing one's sense of (particularistic) identity in a sea of (universalistic) values, even when those values are seen as most desirable, is a sentiment expressed by members of both the majority group and minority constituencies. In the latter case, there is often an added dimension to the support for particularistic identities, since recognizing the host society's national heritage and distinct character provides minority groups with the grounds for asking, in turn, for their distinctiveness to be recognized. Fadia Nassr (2007), Montréal resident and self-described Christian immigrant from Syria, criticizes what she sees as attempts to marginalize religion in contemporary Québec, which she believes have resulted in undermining the collective sense of identity: 'Today, our society shows signs of a weakening of its identity and values, and seems lost in a labyrinth ... In a few years we will see a society that is truly lost, where people could not know themselves, a society who has lost its identity in the name of secularism' (3).[21] The appeal of a strong sense of identity, particularly in the context of growing globalization, is also expressed in a brief by John Saywell (2007), a self-described immigrant to Québec from British Columbia: 'Outside the metropolis, Québec is more homogeneous, breeds more of the so-called old-stock traditions, isolates and protects itself against the cultural ravages of globalization. What it loses through lack of diversity, it gains in integrity. Québec therefore has the best of both worlds because it has in itself the means to recognize and retain its soul, while opening itself onto a world in evolution' (5).[22] For Yara El-Ghadban (2007), a Palestinian Québecer, recognition of particularistic identities is crucial as a measure against erasure by the majoritarian culture. Responding to what she sees as the reductive focus in the Commission's Consultation Document on immigrants as an economic necessity, El-Ghadban calls in her brief for a fuller acknowledgement of the encounter with the Other – the First Nations, the French, the English, the immigrant – which constitutes Québec history, and an inscription in Québec history of 'the history of each of these peoples' (5).[23] The title of El-Ghadban's brief, 'Living the "I Remember" in the Plural,' already suggests the complex reconciliation she wishes to bring about: between the pull of a strong particularistic identity that is also, inescapably, past-oriented (as captured by the emblematic inscription on Québec license plates, 'Je me souviens,' alluded to in the title), and the desire for an open-ended and future-oriented plurality. Her brief, too, like others cited in this chapter, is haunted by the fear of identitarian annihilation. Her concluding section, entitled, 'Diversity has never annihilated peoples' (14),[24] moves back and forth between two conflicting impulses: a sympathy, perhaps particularly heartfelt as a Palestinian, with a host nation struggling to safeguard its survival, and a call for openness to change, and for mixing and heterogeneity, which she finds exemplified in the trope of a mixed marriage.

The model of a mixed marriage, whatever the terms of that mixture, does seem to have the potential to complicate and unsettle the homogeneous and linear narrative of familial descent that informs nation discourse. Hélène Greffard (2006), who identifies herself as a social worker working with recent immigrants in the CLSC Parc Extension, entitles her brief, 'An old-stock Québécois's journey in foreign lands.' The brief opens with her 'credentials' as an old-stock Québécois, the familiar recitation of ancestral history: 'Born in Québec, I am, as we say, an old-stock Québécois. My French ancestor, Louis Greffard, settled in Ile d'Orléans around 1650. He married a young woman born in that new colony. There followed many generations until my father. The latter, born in Sainte-Anne-de-Beaupré, lived all his life in Québec. His work led him to survey the entire Québec territory. He belonged to this breed of men who were "runners of the woods" and builders of this country' (3).[25] Growing up in Québec, her world was to all appearances white, French-speaking, and Catholic. Yet, it also contained differences, beginning with her English-speaking cousins from her mother's Franco-Ontarian side of the family, and including the differently colored porters she would see as a child travelling by train to visit the family in Ontario, and members of First Nations and Inuit communities her father would come into contact with in his work as a surveyor. Coming to Montréal and working with immigrants, Greffard writes, has further opened up her world and irrevocably transformed her vision. It has taught her a number of lessons: that one never knows the other; that coming to know another – of one's own familiar group as much as others – is always a process of getting to know them, for 'aren't human beings a complex system in perpetual change?' (8);[26] that one's perception of the world is the product of one's upbringing and education; that such a frame of reference only appears natural and inevitable but can in effect be suspended in order to explore other options; that one has a choice between 'seeking comfort in one's certitudes or being at ease with the infinite forms reality takes' (11).[27] Greffard clearly opts for the latter, and the resulting vision is one that is not national but planetary in scope. Each person she meets, she writes, reveals to her 'another facet of our planet' (14).[28]

The first-person plural here strives for the broadest human community, affirming that 'we are all linked and in the same boat, part of one immense chain,' and thus 'whatever happens to any one of us affects all the rest' (Greffard 2006: 15).[29] Such a planetary frame of reference also informs the brief by Benoît Gignac (2007) of Saint-Sauveur, who presents his 'idealist' vision of a Québec that dares to be truly different by shedding all particularistic attachments: 'Well if Québec is so different, it's a bit too early to tell, it can prove it by becoming the first planetary community to rid itself of territorial, national, cultural and religious concepts on the basis of which the world has so poorly constructed itself since the dawn of time. Let us accept the existential fact that we are all nomads, Métis in search of a land of refuge where one could find love, work, food, rest and pure air. Let us find what could unite us beyond language and a flag. Let us accept the fact that we are always in movement and that it is dangerous to seek to define "us" once and for all. As if that could be done. The only points of departure and arrival of our existence are those of our birth and anticipated progeny. For that to continue to happen, let us build the first planetary community in the world, and most importantly let us not impose on it any borders' (4).[30]

Interestingly, a planetary frame of reference also informs another 'idealist' narrative – Environics president Michael Adams' *Unlikely Utopia: The Surprising Triumph of Canadian Pluralism* – published in the months leading up to the Bouchard-Taylor Commission and written in the context of the Hérouxville incident and others that fuelled the reasonable accommodation debate. Referring to the analysis offered by commentators such as Andrew Cohen (cited at the beginning of this chapter) of the identity crisis currently plaguing Western countries, Adams (2007) retorts that 'not all identity crises are the same' (39). In the case of Canada, he argues, diversity has always been an indisputable fact on the ground, and drawing on polls and surveys he suggests that, 'the paradox of Canadian chauvinism' is precisely the recognition of the moral superiority of not possessing 'some core identity worth forcing others into' (37–8). The result is a broad and deep popular support for multiculturalism understood not so much as an identitarian doctrine, but as a manner of 'living in a diverse, just, and peaceful society' (41). Canadians, Adams concludes, are 'on our way to becoming the planet's experts in the quiet heroism of getting along' (42).

I have argued that the briefs submitted to the Bouchard-Taylor Commission demonstrate that imagining collective identity in Québec today occurs within, and occasionally against, the framework of nation discourse. Québec citizens of the twenty-first century seem by and large to endorse a set of common civic values meant to protect human rights and freedoms, but it becomes evident that the appeal of such universalist values – which by definition are inclusive, non-discriminating (making no distinctions), and thus indifferent to, if not at odds with, the exclusive categories that constitute particularistic identities – pales in comparison to the powerful pull of identity narratives and the affectively charged promise of belonging they carry. Both the commissioner's Consultation Document – intended to set the terms of the debate – and the briefs submitted by individuals and organizations, indicate that at the present time the conversation about collective identity in Québec is framed by an acceptance of a discourse of peoplehood, with briefs by self-identified old-stock Québécois and Aboriginal individuals effectively mirroring each other in their sense of an historical and cultural distinctiveness, their concern for the future of the collectivity, and their demands for collective rights. In Bouchard and Taylor's formulation, the challenge faced by Québec's model of interculturalism lies in reconciling two conflicting elements: respect for diversity and the imperatives of collective integration. My argument here has been that what the massive archive generated by the Commission suggests is that the conflict that haunts interculturalism in Québec is rather between two rival models of community: nation (premised on peoplehood) and citizenship. It remains to be seen whether a similar exercise in other parts of Canada would reveal the different results of a multiculturalist model that, according to some, in effect underplays ethnocultural identity as it seeks to promote a sense of belonging to a civicist political community invested not in particularistic identities but in a search for commonly shared civic values.[31]

5 The B-T Report 'Open Secularism' Model and the Supreme Court of Canada Decisions on Freedom of Religion and Religious Accommodation

JOSÉ WOEHRLING

Introduction

One of the key themes of the public debate that took place as part of the Bouchard-Taylor Commission in the fall of 2007 concerned 'laïcité' (*secularism* is the best, but still inadequate, available translation). Various participants asked the commissioners to propose the adoption of a principle of secularism based on the French model that would serve to set better guidelines for the practice of religious accommodation, and, in a more general way, to better define the place of religion in the social sphere. The Commission's report does in fact take a position on this question by devoting an extensive chapter to it: chapter VII, entitled 'The Québec System of Secularism' (Bouchard and Taylor 2008: 130–54). As this title indicates, the Commission considers that there is already a secular model being applied in Québec, even though historically it has been defined in an implicit rather than explicit manner. It is the Commission's view that this model, which it qualifies as 'open' secularism, does not require any major modification but rather deserves to be made explicit, further developed, and, in certain respects, clarified. In this chapter I therefore first intend to examine the reasons why the Commission chose to reject the model of 'rigid' secularism proposed by some participants who were hostile to religious accommodation, and to declare itself in favour of an 'open' secularism that is compatible with such accommodation. Secondly, I will look at the extent to which this model proposed by the Commission is compatible with the case-law of the Canadian Supreme Court with respect to religious freedom and religious accommodation.

'Open Secularism' versus 'Rigid Secularism'

In its report, the Bouchard-Taylor Commission takes a stand regarding two models of secularism: on the one hand, the stricter one inspired by the French model put forward by certain participants hostile to religious accommodation; and, on the other, the more liberal and tolerant model which the Commission sees as already being implicitly applied in Québec and that it refers to as 'open secularism.' These two models distinguish themselves by their interpretation of the various constituent facets of secularism, as well as by the respective importance given to each of these components. The four key principles constituting any model of secularism are, according to the Commission: freedom of conscience and religion; the right of individuals to religious and moral equality, without discrimination (direct or indirect), based on convictions of conscience or religious convictions; the separation of church and state; state neutrality towards religion.

According to the Commission, the first two principles define the final purposes of secularism. The other two find their expression more in the institutional structures that are needed to achieve these purposes; however, they can be defined in different ways and prove to be more or less permissive or restrictive from the standpoint of religious practice (Bouchard-Taylor 2008: 135–6).[1] Comparative observation shows that in each national context, secularism can take on a different meaning depending on the importance given to each of these four principles. A more 'strict' or 'rigid' secularism would give more importance to the principle of neutrality than to freedom of conscience and religion, thus allowing a greater restriction of the practice of religion in the name of neutrality, and a separation between political and religious power (for example, by prohibiting the wearing of religious signs by all government employees). A more 'flexible' or more 'open' secularism, on the other hand, would be based on the protection of freedom of religion, even if this calls for the relativization of the principle of neutrality (for example, by authorizing the wearing of religious signs by government employees, or at least by most of them).

The Rejection of the Model of 'Rigid' Secularism[2]

The Commission's report refers to this model as 'rigid secularism,' and underscores the fact that it is inspired by the French model. It points out, however, that those who promote it in Québec do not fully understand the complexity of true French secularism and have a simplistic and distorted image of what it is. Thus the report underlines the fact that while France has prohibited the wearing of 'conspicuous' religious signs by students in public primary and secondary schools, the state continues, on the other hand, to take charge of the maintenance of Catholic, Protestant, and Jewish religious buildings constructed before the adoption of the Law Concerning the Separation of Church and State of 1905, and that it substantially subsidizes private religious schools under contract with the government.[3]

According to the Commission, the characteristics of 'rigid secularism' are the following:

First, this form of secularism has the status of an explicit and autonomous constitutional principle (as we will see further on; at the present time neither the Canadian Constitution nor the Québec laws contain any explicit recognition of a principle of secularism).[4]

Second, the aims of this form of secularism go beyond just the promotion of moral and religious equality and individual freedom of conscience and religion. It has been given the mission to carry out the emancipation of individuals with respect to religion; in other words, the secularization or erosion of religious belief, or, at the least, the relegation of religious practice to private and community life. This kind of conception of secularism is thus based on a negative opinion of religion which sees religion as incompatible with individual autonomy and rationality.

The Commission finds this conception to be highly problematic in the sense that it 'adheres to atheists' and agnostics' conception of the world, and of good, and consequently does not treat with equal consideration citizens who make a place for religion in their system of beliefs and values' (Bouchard and Taylor 2008: 138). The autonomy of individuals requires that they have the means to make their own choices regarding fundamental values, whether these choices are secular, religious, or spiritual in nature.

Promoters of such a 'rigid' secularism model also see it as necessary for facilitating civic integration (understood as an allegiance to a common civic identity) by means of neutralizing religion as an identity marker that serves to differentiate individuals. This position, often described as 'republican' by its adherents, supposes that the removal of differences (like those emanating from religion or ethnicity) is a prerequisite condition for civic integration. From the Commission's perspective, this idea is disputable, and it prefers the view that mutual understanding and cooperation between citizens of a diversified society 'demand, to the contrary, that their […] differences be recognized and respected' (Bouchard and Taylor 2008: 138).

Third, this strict form of secularism is understood as being applied not only to public institutions, but also to individuals themselves when using public institutions, or even, for the most radical 'secularists,' to public space in general. This means that this kind of secularism has the effect of prohibiting individuals from using public services, and, even more so, employees in public institutions (public agents) from wearing any visible religious signs. According to this conception of secularism, the practice of religion must be relegated to the private and communal sphere, and the 'public sphere' must remain exempt of any expression of religion.

In the Commission's view, such an approach is derived from an erroneous understanding of the distinction between the 'private' and the 'public' spheres regarding the place of religion in society. While it is true that 'public' institutions must obey the principle of religious neutrality, in so far as they are under the authority of the various levels of government (federal, provincial, and municipal), the same requirement for neutrality obviously does not apply to individuals who are, on the contrary, free to express their religious and moral convictions as much in private as in 'public' (meaning in public spaces that are 'open to the public' and accessible to all members of the civil society, such as streets, parks, businesses, and various associations).[5] This distinction between the two meanings of the concept of 'public sphere' allows us to understand why the same principles of individual religious freedom and state religious neutrality prohibit a public school from offering a denominational (rather than cultural) teaching of religion, or from establishing the recitation of prayers before the beginning of classes, but allow students attending this school to display religious signs. It is only if we confuse these two meanings of 'public sphere' that we would see a paradox in this situation.

Finally, it is clear that the model of strict or 'rigid' secularism is not compatible with religious accommodation, which aims precisely to foster the free exercise of religion by eliminating certain obstacles that hinder it.[6] From this perspective, accommodation, to the extent that it 'helps' religious practice, is incompatible with the state's duty to religious neutrality and the goal of ensuring the emancipation of individuals with respect to religion.

For the Bouchard-Taylor Commission, this model of strict secularism is not appropriate for Québec because it does not allow the four constituent principles of secularism to be implemented in an acceptable manner. It carries out the separation of church and state, and, in one possible way, the state's duty of neutrality, but it does not sufficiently protect religious freedom and equality. Thus, for example, the prohibition against wearing visible religious signs in public institutions, even if applied uniformly to all users or all employees of these institutions, discriminates against those (and only those) whose religious convictions require the wearing of such signs.

'Open' Secularism

In the Commission's view, the model of secularism currently applied in Québec, which it refers to as 'open secularism,' should be preserved, precisely because it permits the optimal reconciliation of the four constituent facets of secularism.[7] This model, which has never received *explicit* legislative or constitutional recognition (and is therefore applied in an implicit manner), was gradually implemented in response to a series of historical events and political decisions that are recounted in the Commission's report (Bouchard and Taylor 2008: 139–40).

Contrary to a rather widespread belief, this process of secularization did not begin with the 'Quiet Revolution' of the 1960s, although its pace quickened during that period. According to the Commission, it is mainly the institutionalization of the culture of rights and freedoms, with the adoption of the charters of rights (first the Québec Charter of 1977, then the Canadian Charter in 1982), which established and deepened the secularism of Québec's public institutions.

The Commission also notes that in the 1990s and since the year 2000, before the beginning of the reasonable accommodation controversy, the debate in Québec about secularism focused mainly on the status of public schools. One should remember that the denominational status of part of the Québec public school system was entrenched in the Canadian Constitution, more precisely in Section 93 of the Constitution Act of 1867.[8] The amendment of Article 93 in 1997 by a bilateral constitutional amendment (approved by the federal and Québec authorities) permitted the Québec school system to become non-denominational (it is now organized along linguistic, rather than religious, lines).[9] However, Catholic and Protestant denominational teaching was maintained in the public schools by having recourse to the notwithstanding clause, which allows derogation of the Québec and Canadian Charters. This denominational teaching would disappear in July 2008 and be replaced with the teaching of ethics and religious culture, which in turn would allow for the termination of the notwithstanding clause.

According to the Commission, the characteristics of the 'open' model of secularism are the following (we can see that they are opposed point by point to the characteristics of strict secularism):

First, within such an 'open' model, secularism is not an explicit and autonomous constitutional principle ('an overhanging principle'); it is rather 'an institutional arrangement that is aimed at protecting rights and freedoms' (Bouchard and Taylor 2008: 141). State neutrality towards religion and separation of church and state are not seen as ends in themselves, but as means to achieve the fundamental twofold objective: respect for religious and moral equality, and freedom of conscience and religion. In other words, if there is tension or contradiction between the various constituent facets of secularism, this tension should be resolved in favour of religious freedom and equality and not in favour of separation or neutrality. More specifically, if there is an apparent contradiction between religious accommodations and religious neutrality of the state, neutrality must yield to the accommodations.

Second, open secularism neither strives to further secularization or erosion of religious belief, nor does it serve to neutralize or erase religion as an identity marker (contrary to the model of 'republican' secularism, which does aim to do all of the above).

Third, open secularism is directed at state institutions, but not at individuals who use these institutions or even work in them as employees. In order to illustrate the consequences of this model of secularism, the Commission examines a question that kept coming up during the Québec public debate in the autumn of 2007: the wearing of religious signs by government employees during the exercising of their functions.

It begins by noting that this question does not pose any difficulty for the supporters of strict secularism of the 'republican' kind: in this model a general rule of prohibition applies to all agents of the state, even those who do simple technical work and who are not in contact with the public. (This is the situation that exists in France, for example.)[10]

On the other hand, this question is more difficult for the open secularism model, which attempts to reconcile the demands of freedom of religion and conscience of public employees with those of religious neutrality of public institutions (because public agents represent the state and should in principle embrace the values promoted by the state).[11] The Commission's report (2008) presents all the arguments for and against the various solutions that could conceivably be adopted regarding this problem, and finally concludes that a uniform prohibition applied to all public employees, whatever the nature of their functions, would be exaggerated and unjustifiable, but that a limited prohibition is justified in the case of public agents that hold positions 'that embody [...] the necessary neutrality of the State' (151), which applies, according to the report, to the president and vice-presidents of the National Assembly, to judges and Crown prosecutors, and lastly to police officers and prison guards. One suspects that by recommending this special treatment for certain categories of public agents, the Commission is not so much applying the principles of open secularism as attempting to satisfy, at least partially, Québec public opinion, which includes a large segment in favour of a general ban on the wearing of religious signs by public agents.

It is difficult to say whether the prohibition of religious signs for some categories of public agents would be validated or invalidated by the courts. There does exist a decision of the Federal Court of Canada, in the *Grant* case of 1995, which touches upon this question; however, at that time the Court had to decide, not whether freedom of religion allows the prohibition of the wearing of religious signs by the members of the Royal Canadian Mounted Police, but rather to the contrary, if it prohibits the permitting of it. In fact, in this case, an association of retired members of the Royal Canadian Mounted Police invoked the Canadian Charter to contest a decision by the RCMP commissioner to allow Sikhs to serve as members of the RCMP while wearing a turban instead of the traditional felt Stetson hat. The association invoked freedom of religion and claimed that the wearing of a visible religious sign by a police officer could violate the religious freedom of those individuals coming into contact with him. The Federal Court, however, rejected this claim.[12]

If we turn to comparative law and politics, the situation in the United States and in Germany shows that in a federal state, it is not necessary for such a question to be resolved in an absolutely uniform manner, even when applying rights and freedoms guaranteed by the federal constitution. The American Supreme Court and the German Constitutional Court accept that the states and *länder* can choose between authorizing and prohibiting the wearing of religious signs by teachers in public schools.[13] In the hypothetical case where Québec would adopt solutions in this area that are different from those being applied in other provinces, it remains to be seen whether the Canadian Supreme Court would allow the provinces a certain margin of appreciation, or if it would rather adopt a position that says that freedom of religion guaranteed in the Canadian Charter must be interpreted in the same way all across the country.[14]

Convergence of 'Open' Secularism and Canadian Case-Law

To begin with, it is useful to note that there are few decisions in which the Supreme Court has expressed a position on the concept of secularism, or, rather, since this concept does not exist as such in Canadian constitutional law, on the related concept of religious neutrality of the state. This can be explained in large part by the fact that neither the Canadian Constitution in its entirety nor the Canadian Charter of Rights and Freedoms, in particular, contains any explicit principle of religious neutrality of the state, whereas the French Constitution of 1958 has its principle of secularism (laïcité),[15] and the Constitution of the United States has its principle of 'non-establishment' as part of the First Amendment.[16]

The Canadian Supreme Court has nevertheless discovered a duty of religious neutrality of the state implicitly contained in the Canadian Charter, recognizing that this duty is a logical consequence of the freedom of religion as well as of religious equality, which it also recognized as being indirectly guaranteed by Article 2a of the Charter.[17] In fact, the Court ruled in the first decision that it rendered under Section 2a (the *Big M Drug Mart* decision of 1985) that the federal Sunday Act, to the extent that it imposed the respect of Sunday on all Canadians *for religious reasons*, created an inequality with respect to non-Christians, as well as infringing on their freedom of religion by subjecting them to a form of coercion. In this case, the Attorney General for Canada defended the validity of the law by pointing out that, contrary to the American First Amendment, Section 2a of the Canadian Charter does not contain an explicit 'non-establishment clause,' and claimed that the only possible conclusion is that protection of religious freedom in Canada is aimed only at free exercise. The Supreme Court nevertheless gave effect to the existence of the neutrality principle in ruling as unconstitutional the Sunday Act because it had a religious and not a secular objective.[18]

Furthermore, two later decisions of the Ontario Court of Appeal illustrate the consequences of this duty of neutrality in the context of public education. In *Zylberberg*,[19] the Court ruled that a school regulation was incompatible with Section 2a of the Canadian Charter insofar as it made provision for the recitation of Christian prayers in public school, despite the fact that parents had the possibility, if they so desired, to obtain an exemption for their children. The view of the Court was that the regulation exerted a form of indirect pressure on the parents and students to conform to the religious behaviour of the majority, which would, in practice, make them hesitate to claim the benefit of the exemption. In another case, involving the *Canadian Civil Liberties Association*,[20] the same Court of Appeal found that a regulation adopted under Ontario's Education Act, which made provision for religious instruction in public schools unless parents asked for an exemption, was a violation of religious freedom. The Court considered that the exemption available to parents could not save the regulation, given that the pressure of conformity could dissuade certain parents from claiming the exemption for fear of being socially stigmatized.[21] At the same time the Court insisted on the difference between, on the one hand, religious *instruction* that is aimed at indoctrination into a particular religion and that violates freedom of religion; and, on the other, religious *education*, meaning the pluralistic teaching of religions, which is constitutionally permitted in public schools.[22]

Citing these two decisions of the Ontario Court of Appeal, Judge Sopinka of the Canadian Supreme Court affirmed in the *Adler* case[23] that 'This secular nature [of the public school system] is itself mandated by s. 2a of the *Charter*, as held by several courts in this country.' In other words, the Charter requires that public schools be secular, that is, they must respect the principle of neutrality.

Finally, more recently, in the *Village de Lafontaine* case,[24] Judge LeBel (speaking on his own behalf as well as on behalf of Judges Bastarache and Deschamps) examined, in *obiter dictum*, the question of the existence and of the significance of a duty of religious neutrality of the state as a constituent facet of freedom of religion guaranteed by the Canadian Charter. Here is what Judge LeBel has to say on this question: 'This fundamental freedom [freedom of religion] imposes on the state and public authorities, in relation to all religions and citizens, a duty of religious neutrality that assures individual or collective tolerance, thereby safeguarding the dignity of every individual and ensuring equality for all.'[25]

As we can see, the principle of state religious neutrality has not as yet been the subject of any systematic and comprehensive discussion by the highest court in Canada. In this respect, we can imagine that the importance given by the Bouchard-Taylor Commission to this discussion, as it relates to the various models of secularism, will perhaps give the Supreme Court an occasion to delve more deeply into this subject in future cases dealing with freedom of religion.

Yet, even if the principle of state religious neutrality has not been the subject of an in-depth study by the Supreme Court, it is nonetheless possible to compare the views of the Court with the principle of open secularism advocated by the Bouchard-Taylor Commission, and thus observe whether the two are essentially similar.

As is the case with the Commission's open secularism, the principle of neutrality recognized by the Supreme Court does not have an autonomous constitutional existence, but rather constitutes a mere means to protect freedom of conscience and religion as well as individuals' religious and moral equality. Indeed, a look at constitutional comparative law shows that in order to impose a duty of religious neutrality on the state, the courts can either base themselves on an autonomous principle of neutrality explicitly recognized as such, or, when such a principle is not part of the constitutional text, as in the Canadian Charter, they can invoke religious freedom and equality as the source of an implicit principle of religious state neutrality. In the first case, any significant state support of a religion could be considered prohibited; consequently, the duty of neutrality, founded on an autonomous constitutional principle, would tend to be rigorous, as seen, for example, in the United States. On the other hand, in the second case, if the duty of neutrality follows from the principle of religious equality and the right to the free exercise of religion, it would be necessary to demonstrate, in order to contest the support given by the state to a particular religion, that such support has discriminatory aspects or else that it creates social coercion that significantly limits the freedom of religion of those who do not adhere to this religion.

Yet, not all forms of state support for a religion have such an effect. Some forms foster the exercise of some people's religious freedom without limiting that of others. As we have seen previously, Canadian courts ruled that prayers and religious instruction organized by school authorities in public schools restricted freedom of religion in an unjustifiable manner, even if there was the possibility of exemption, because the fact of having to ask for it would risk creating stigmatization by peers, and, consequently, an indirect coercion on students and their parents.[26] Thus, in this case, the duty of neutrality entails the necessity to put an end to this form of religious expression, to the extent that this is the result of an initiative of school authorities themselves. On the other hand, the courts also ruled that freedom of religion imposed a duty of accommodation on public schools, regarding, for example, school holidays and the wearing of religious signs. Here, consequently, the principle of neutrality does not oppose religious displays in school, as long as these are the result of the students' own initiatives and constitute a form of exercising their religious freedom. In other words, as with the open secularism proposed by the Bouchard-Taylor Commission, religious neutrality, as recognized by Canadian courts, is imposed on the state and public authorities but is not imposed on individuals.

And so we can see that the duty of neutrality that is sourced in the principle of religious equality and in freedom of religion will be less rigorous than the one based on an autonomous and explicit principle of neutrality. Such a relativist interpretation is even more appropriate in the case of the Canadian Constitution because of the existence of Section 93 of the Constitution Act of 1867, which entrenches certain confessional rights for Catholics and Protestants in the area of education.[27] The principle of neutrality is therefore necessarily less rigorous in Canada than in the United States.[28] In the United States, the non-establishment clause has been interpreted as prohibiting any direct financial aid from the state to confessional schools. In Canada, however, the principle of religious neutrality issuing from freedom of religion should not be understood as preventing the state from financially assisting confessional schools, as long as it is done without favouring any one religion over another.[29]

Finally, like the Bouchard-Taylor Commission, the Supreme Court is of the view that the principle of neutrality is not opposed to religious accommodation. On the contrary, it considers that a duty of religious accommodation follows from the constitutional protection of religious freedom and equality.

In the *Big M Drug Mart* and *Edwards Books* cases, the Supreme Court recognized that when a law that pursues a valid secular objective entails some restrictive effects on the religious freedom of certain individuals, these individuals have the right to obtain an accommodation, notably in the form of an exemption from the application of the law, on condition that such a solution is compatible with the public interest. The exemption will be refused if the government succeeds in demonstrating that it is necessary for the law in question to be applied without exception, or, as in the *Edwards Books* case, without any additional exemption to those already provided by the legislature.[30] In this case it was the Retail Business Holidays Act of Ontario, which prohibited the opening of retail stores on Sunday, that was being contested. The exemptions granted by the law were directed only at small-scale businesses that closed on Saturdays. Faced with the same question prior to the Supreme Court, the Ontario Court of Appeal, in *R. v. Videoflicks Ltd*,[31] had arrived at the conclusion that the law infringed on the religious freedom of retail owners of the Jewish faith, who could not (because of the size of their businesses) take advantage of the exceptions allowed in the law, and, in order to sincerely follow the precepts of their religion, did not open on Saturday. The Court thus ruled that the law was *of no force as to them*, which led to these individuals being granted a 'constitutional exemption' with respect to the law inasmuch as it violated their freedom of religion.

This decision of the Ontario Court of Appeal was overturned by the Supreme Court in the *Edwards Books* ruling. The majority of the Court ruled that the law was valid without any exemptions having to be added to those already provided by the legislature. The Court began by recognizing that the secular objective of the law, that is, to establish a weekly day of rest that would be the same for all workers, was valid. However, the law restricted the religious freedom of those who observed the Sabbath by imposing on them an added financial burden, as they had to close their businesses for one day more than those who observe Sunday as a religious day. While recognizing that the Ontario legislature was required to accommodate, as much as possible, those obliged by their religion to close on a day other than Sunday, the majority of the Court considered that the exemptions already granted in the law constituted a sufficient accommodation, and that the addition of supplementary exemptions would endanger the effectiveness of the legislative measures in question. To the contrary, the Court of Appeal had ruled that the law had not gone far enough in the direction of accommodation, and that it should have accorded the exemption to all business owners who close on Saturday for religious reasons, whatever the size of the business. Let us note that subsequently, the Ontario government, on its own initiative, modified the law to extend the Sabbatarian exemption to all businesses, whatever their size, that close on any day other than Sunday for religious reasons.

Conclusion

We can now sum up by stating that the model of secularism advocated by the Bouchard-Taylor Report is essentially the same as the one applied by Canadian courts in their interpretation of the Canadian Charter of Rights and Freedoms (in the name of state religious neutrality). This similarity with the Canadian model undoubtedly explains, at least in part, the Québec nationalists' negative reaction to this section of the report. They would have preferred that the Commission propose the adoption by Québec of a model of secularism clearly distinct from the Canadian model. The Parti Québécois and the Action démocratique du Québec were very critical of the concept of open secularism, judging it as not 'republican' enough. As for the provincial government formed by the Québec Liberal Party, it claims to approve, in a general way, the concept of open secularism; however, the day after the publication of the report, Premier Charest rushed to get the unanimous adoption by the National Assembly of a resolution to reject the recommendation of the report concerning the removal of the crucifix from the National Assembly.[32]

Furthermore, the reaction of public opinion to the concept of 'open' secularism was also negative for other reasons. The public reacted negatively to the proposition that, on the one hand, public employees (with a few exceptions) be allowed to wear their religious signs during the exercise of their functions, and, on the other, that the crucifix hanging above the president's chair in the National Assembly be removed. Some Québecers felt that this was equal to banishing the religious symbols of the majority, while at the same time allowing those of minorities to enter the public sphere.

As was pointed out earlier, this apparently paradoxical result is explained by the principles upheld by the Commission, which are the same as those found in the jurisprudence of the Supreme Court. On the one hand, behaviour or expressions of a religious nature initiated by public authorities are subject to the principle of state religious neutrality. This duty of neutrality has been interpreted in a rather strict manner by Canadian courts, so much so that, in general, the religious behaviour and expressions that public authorities could initiate are prohibited, or at least narrowly restricted, precisely to the extent that they are considered to be likely to exert unacceptable coercion on individuals, and, by favouring certain religions, to be discriminatory as well. On the other hand, in instances where the behaviour or expressions are initiated by individuals, they are a matter of religious freedom; that is, the freedom of these individuals to express their religious convictions through certain practices, and their right not to be subjected to direct or indirect religious discrimination because of that. If such a right comes into conflict with secular and neutral laws or regulations (i.e., those that do not aim at promoting or prohibiting a religious belief or practice), the public authorities find it their duty to accommodate unless they can show that the accommodation in question would entail an excessive constraint for the public interest. One must realize that the combination and application of the principles that we have expounded here are complex and difficult to explain and to justify to public opinion.

Finally, it can be noted that the Bouchard-Taylor Report considered unnecessary, contrary to what some have suggested, to adopt a new legislative instrument to clarify the terms of secularism, or to modify the Charter of Human Rights and Freedoms (Québec Charter) to include this principle. It suggests, rather, that the Québec government publish a White Paper on secularism, which would then be put before the National Assembly, the purpose of which would be to clarify the founding principles and purposes of the Québec model of secularism and to provide citizens with a tool that could help structure public discussion on this subject.

6 Conclusion: Religion, Culture, and the State

HOWARD ADELMAN

Introduction

Newcomers should give up their cultural traditions and become more like everybody else. This was the position of a majority of Québecers polled by Léger Marketing for the Association for Canadian Studies[1] a year after Bouchard and Taylor released their report. Further, the trend line of anxiety about and resistance to incorporating other cultures became worse in the year after the B-T Report came out. Forty per cent of francophones viewed non-Christian immigrants as a threat to Québec society, compared with 32 per cent in 2007, while only 32 per cent of non-francophones harboured the same fears, a figure that *declined* compared with 34 per cent in 2007. B-T clearly did not change the attitudes of francophone, allophone, or anglophone Québecers, except perhaps to exacerbate Québécois' fears.

Why did this occur? Why the enhanced anxiety? Some explain minority fears in terms of group economic insecurity. Antonius Rachad argued that 'Focusing on cultural differences is the wrong approach.'[2] What minorities really want and need is both equality of opportunity and results. Economic integration produces change.

But the polls suggest other more important factors – age, for example. Fifty-six per cent of 18- to 24-year-olds polled approved wearing hijābs in public schools, but only 30 per cent of those 55 and over agreed. The linguistic group to which an individual belongs also counts. Sixty-three per cent of non-francophones approve wearing headscarves in public schools, but only 32 per cent of French-speakers agreed. And only 25 per cent of francophones thought they had a responsibility to make a greater effort to accept minority groups' customs, while 74 per cent of non-francophones thought they should make a greater effort.

One clue is that Québec is only superficially secular, for only half of Québécois approved a non-denominational course on ethics and religion while 78 per cent of non-francophones approved of the course. Further, given our chapter on Jews in Québec, the poll is perhaps more ominous: 88 per cent of French-speakers viewed Catholics favourably, while 60 per cent viewed Jews favourably, and that number had dropped 12 points since the Bouchard-Taylor Report was released. More importantly, 36 per cent of Québecers viewed Judaism unfavourably. Only 40 per cent had a positive attitude towards Muslims, down 17 per cent before Bouchard and Taylor made their comparison, when 57 per cent in 2007 were positively disposed. In contrast, among non-francophones, 92 per cent viewed Catholics with favour, 77 per cent had a positive opinion of Jews, and 65 per cent had a good opinion of Muslims. This suggests a closer analysis of the resistance to change of *de souche*, old-stock Québécois.

On the other hand, the Bouchard-Taylor Report showed that in actual practice Québecers had no trouble at all in reasonably accommodating the needs of minorities. So what lies behind these discrepancies between actual practices versus generalized attitudes? In the tension between religion and secularism discussed in B-T and in the chapters in this volume that analyse open and closed secularism; in the friction between religious, ethnic, and nationalist communitarianism versus the universal principles of human rights based on individualism; and in all the other strains and stresses – between the old and the young, between the less and the more educated, between those attached to locality and group versus those with a global world outlook – Bouchard and Taylor tried to find a balance. Our contributors have explored that balance, as well as the unique way it is being forged in Québec, cast midway between the either/or formula of France and the relatively relaxed attitudes of the ROC (rest of Canada) and the USA.

Clearly, Québec religious, ethnic, and nationalist traditions play a powerful role. Bina Toledo Freiwald brought that out very clearly in her analysis of the submissions made to the Bouchard-Taylor Commission. Québécois are very proud of their traditions, and Premier Jean Charest was quick to reject the Commission's recommendation that the cross behind the Speaker's chair in the provincial parliament be removed. Historically, Québec was a small-scale organic society where day-to-day interpersonal relations count. On that level, treating people rudely if you know them personally is unacceptable. There is a radical separation between what someone might think of the Other's religion or ethnicity and how they are to be treated individually. Negative behaviour towards real persons is not the same as negative attitudes to the group to which they might belong. That is the irony. Québéois communitarianism demands that *individuals* be respected. This attitude, rooted in heritage, especially in small francophone rural milieus, remains constant almost to this day, even in Montreal. The Québéois may be an imaginary community in Anderson's (1991) sense, but it is also far more than that, for it is rooted in history and experience, customs and practices developed over time.

The reality is that communitarianism has been a dominant foundation for Québec values, providing a paramount influence on personal communications. This remains a deep underlying current. Notions of individualism and individual rights are a relatively superficial and recent accretion. The survey results with which this chapter began, and the Bouchard-Taylor Report, reveal that as francophone identity is threatened, Québéois are little different than most groups. The media circus of the Bouchard-Taylor Commission stirred up those fears. In proportion to their personal insecurities, suspicion of the Other increases whether those others be Jews or Muslims, and their trust in themselves decreases. This is all reinforced by their self-identity as an enlarged version of a Canada-wide identity of themselves as losers – beautiful losers, but losers nonetheless – in the face of more powerful forces of modernization and globalization.

> [T]he belief that the rights of the community can trump the rights of the individual – and that this is not incompatible with liberalism but exactly what humanizes it – really is a distinctly Canadian intuition. It is argued in different ways, and with different emphasis, by the influential McGill philosopher Charles Taylor ... and by the essayist John Ralston Saul and the Queen's University philosopher Will Kymlicka. (Gopnik 2009a: 30)

How does communitarianism both trump yet become reconciled with the Anglo-American tradition of individual rights embedded in a liberal theory of individual rights? French social contract theory presumes a contract between the state and the individuals who are its citizens, to guarantee those universal rights. In English social contract theory, liberal theory presumes an original state devoid of politics where we are all conceived to be individuals with inborn inherited

Conclusion: Religion, Culture, and the State   103

rights which we cannot and will not surrender to the state even as we join the state to ease our fears. The Americans forged a constitution that pleated together both strands of individual rights so that the citizens inherited a tradition of suspicion of the very same state that guaranteed their individual rights.

But long before the Québec Charter of Human Rights in 1975 and the Canadian Charter of Rights and Freedoms in 1982, Canada had another tradition of individual human rights. It grew out of the soil of Scottish ethnic history combining universal rights with communal preservation by rooting rights, not in nature or social contracts made in a state of nature but in actual social contracts which knit people into communities of expectations, rights, and privileges reinforced by habits and customs so that communitarianism and individualism, rather than being polar opposites, reinforced one another.[3] Canadian communitarianism, the sense of identity and who Canadians are, is a product of Canadian history, of the communities that nurtured and imbued its citizens with their core values. Whereas anti-communitarian individualism claims that communitarianism is at the root of the wild nightmares of exclusivist ethno-nationalist politics, communitarianism declares that non-communitarian individualism is a cold and icy theory that leaves a society without bonds and its members without a sense of belonging, so that those members are prone to the ersatz solidarity of exclusivist nationalism that so easily preys on a society of lost individuals rootless from a loss of a sense of community. Further, it is just an abstraction from how people actually behave.[4]

In his essay on Michael Ignatieff, Gopnik (2009b: 30) went on to write that 'Every country has an obscure theoretical dispute – in America, about the moment when human life begins; in France, about the proper meaning of the term *laicité* that crystallizes some of its deepest preoccupations and, in turn, becomes a code for its practical politics.' In Canada, the key issue is how the competing philosophies of communitarianism and individual rights are reconciled, how ingrown a community can become without violating the rights of its individual members and the duties of individual citizens in the Canadian polity. Multiculturalism provides one formula. Interculturalism provides another. In the unique context of Québec and the distinct place it occupies in Canada and North America, where its history created a particular set of circumstances and a distinct community, the tension between communitarianism and individualism followed a special trajectory. As Michael Ignatieff said in the Gopnik essay, in the end what counts are practices and not theory, and the practices in Québec reveal its character best.

However, the B-T Commission demonstrated that the problem in Québec is created by beliefs not practices, beliefs that are played with and manipulated in distorted stories about what seem to be otherwise sweet and reasonable practices. In interpersonal relations, as in many small and rural cultures, the first categorical imperative requires treating the Other, whatever their background, with respect on an interpersonal level, especially if they are strangers. Québec society inherited that tradition. So one might carry negative stereotypes about a group as an abstraction that shapes your attitudes, but in day-to-day practice, those attitudes do not affect behaviour.

Québec Beliefs

Attitudes are very different than theoretical beliefs, for they are immediate, concrete, and, if stimulated, especially by sensationalized media stories fretting about the security of that communitarian tradition, react reflexively and often unthinkingly. B-T did not alter attitudes. In fact, the process probably made francophones more insecure.

Attitudes are part of our existential community system rooted in our fears and follies, with long historical traces. Canada is a country in which the central idiom is survival rather than laicité. As Margaret Atwood (1972) wrote, survival (and victimhood) have been the central preoccupations of Canadian poetry and fiction. For English Canadians, it was survival against the daunting challenge of a vast country of cold and ice. For French Canadians it was survival of the French culture as a community in a North American English sea. As the B-T Commission documented, francophones in Canada remain fundamentally insecure with respect to their identity and future as a community. No amount of rational discourse can alter that sensibility. To be a francophone in North America means that one necessarily carries a sense of minority status and threat and a memory of past defeat, significantly exacerbated by the challenge of modernization and globalization in which English emerged as the predominant language.

Yet B-T documented that in daily practice, francophones were as reasonable, accommodating, and tolerant as anyone might wish. Why the discrepancy between attitudes and behaviour? One usually expects the reverse – pious statements of tolerance hiding intolerant practices. B-T found highly tolerant practices, but the context included a heightened level of intolerance. There is clearly a disjunction between behaviour and attitudes, but one that does not conform to the usual pattern. Further, the Commission itself was created largely because of a number of misrepresentations of incidents in the press. Were Bouchard and Taylor naïve in believing that if they disclosed the sweet reasonableness of Québecers, attitudes would shift as Québecers began to see themselves in an excellent light?

I have heard or read of the following plausible explanations for this paradoxical outcome:

1. Attitudes reflect deeper abiding fears while conduct shifts in response to reality.
2. Québecers aspire to live in a civic nation, but deeper down inhabit an ethnic nation; communitarianism runs deep in Québec society, whereas individualism and the notion of human rights is a relatively recent and superficial acquisition.
3. French culture differs from English culture; the latter is more empirical while the former bases its rationale on first principles.
4. Québec culture differs from that of the rest of Canada because it is rooted in a mono-religious environment rather than one of religious diversity; Québecers, especially older ones, hanker nostalgically for a singular perspective, and, as a result, laïcité and tolerance for diverse religious expression in public are in tension.
5. While Québecers are prone to follow the French model, anglophone-dominated institutions inhibit this route.
6. Media sensationalize and 'stir the kasha.'
7. Court rulings that fail to take account of both attitudes and conduct miss the mark and exacerbate differences rather than reconcile them.
8. Xenophobia and emotion dominate debate in civil society; dreaming of a res publica as an arena for rational debate is an illusion.
9. The problem arises from isolation of minorities rather than mixing; in France, Muslims living in ghettoes in the suburbs are feared and targeted, while in Montreal the main ethnic group with which there were clashes were the Jewish Hasidim living cheek by jowl in the midst of francophones, a situation exacerbated by the historical legacy of the Catholic view of Jews as Christ-killers.
10. Multiculturalism is the real source of the problem, for it fosters and stirs debate where there need be none if a dominant set of practices of that culture were recognized.

11 Opportunistic politicians always undermine the prospect of a reasonable civil society.
12 The state is in decline with the increasing pace of globalization, so that states best exemplify their strength by resuming violent conflict over differences.

How do we select which among these various interpretations play any role? Will that set of explanations help foster a more liberal approach to migrants and refugees, or need there even be a more liberal approach since the practice in civil society already works? Instead of beginning with an analysis of the relevance of any of the above propositions, I want to suggest a theoretical frame that links ethnonationalism with civic nationalism and the tolerance of minorities. In ignoring the minorities at first, I begin with a discussion of the relationship of religion to politics as a cornerstone for understanding the political frame.

Religion, Culture, and the State: The Importance of Dominant Values

Adam Gopnik (2009a) recently explored the way a politician like Abraham Lincoln (and a scientist like Charles Darwin) dealt with the divine and the human. Two perspectives were adopted by both mid-nineteenth-century figures: a respect for the individuality and dignity of others, and insisting on an evidential base for truth claims. I begin with the latter. Individualistic rights theories are primarily a priori doctrines. Rights are given. They precede history and historical experience and do not follow from that experience in spite of the fact that they are a seventeenth-century invention. Communitarianism is also a doctrine in which the values of the community are embedded in that community and those historical accretions define the self and the way one looks at the world. An evidenced-based doctrine challenges both assumptions, both the priority of abstract first principles and the priority of communal values endorsed by history. An insistence on evidenced-based truth claims does not challenge either individual rights theory or communitarianism so much as provide both with boundary conditions. Whenever rights theories are so at odds with empirical evidence and historical patterns, the rights theories must be bracketed and not the evidence. Similarly, when doctrines of inherited communal values clash with empirical evidence *and* accepted doctrines of universal rights, the communal inheritance of those values must be suspended until and only when evidence is forthcoming to reinforce those inherited values.

Further, not only does an insistence on an evidential foundation for beliefs provide the base for theory, but each of the theories needs to be deconstructed. Individualism divides into two basic doctrines: an individualism of rights and an individualism of respect. The former is directed towards the primacy of the self. The latter is directed towards the primacy of the other. An individualism of respect regards the recognition of the dignity of the other as a primary touchstone. The alternative doctrine of individualism triumphs the self and its interests as it exuberantly trumpets rights over duties. The former provides a foundation for a communitarian society in which the values of other communities are respected as long as they do not fundamentally interfere with the right of one's own community to adhere to its values and support their continuity. The latter provides a foundation for a contractarian society in which only individual rights, and not communal values, are given recognition.

Now, either doctrine can become a secular religion of blind faith when evidence is ignored, distorted, or deliberately bracketed to protect the doctrine. That secular religion can be as doctrinaire and wilfully blind to its own follies as any traditional divine-directed religion. That is why I endorse the B-T support for open versus closed secularism. France provides an example. A doctrinaire approach, whether based on a religious or a secular foundation, is abominable and likely to lead to insensitivity at the very least, and, in extreme situations, persecution of those who transgress the doctrine whether the doctrine is communal or individual, Catholic or Protestant, or whether the writ is inscribed within an institutional authority or the conscience of individuals taken as a universal category. For doctrine, whatever its source, can make us blind to the delight in the infinite variety of human practices.

This is as true for communitarian as for individualist theories. For they, too, divide. There is a self-regarding communitarianism that insists on the primacy of its values to the exclusion of all others. There is also an other-regarding communiarianism that celebrates, appreciates, and respects differences among communities while remaining dedicated to preserving its own inherited and considered values. It is the latter that is fully compatible with an individualist doctrine of respect for others.

The more one regards and respects the other, the less prone one is to slip into doctrinaire stances. The more one looks to evidence to support one's views, the more likely dogma will remain in check. But is not an evidence-based doctrine itself prone to becoming a dogma? What saves an evidence-based doctrine as the source of boundary conditions from its own descent into dogmatism as exemplified in eugenicists and racist pseudo-sciences of the twentieth century? It is the counterpoise to an evidence-based foundation – a roof of humility and self-critique where the dictum to know thyself becomes the mandate to unpack what Michel de Montaigne in his essay 'On Vanity' (XVIII) listed as the tyranny and treachery, injustice and cupidity, cruelty and naïve stupidity, idleness and self idolatry of the individual. When wisdom becomes congenial it must be discomforted. When truths pile up and war with each other like humans in a crowded ship, the ship must be cleansed and only the most vibrant allowed to remain on board.

What remains? Only the different ways each culture engages in the dialectic interplay between these corner posts of evidence and self-criticism, of an individualism and a communitarianism of respect that link together and mediate between an individualism of rights and an understandable ethno-communal determination to survive. There are alternative scenarios in dealing with the tension between beliefs and attitudes. The dialectic can play out in a creative initiative. Secondly, the tension can become encrusted like barnacles on the ship of state. Third, the state can reinforce that encrustation by making one part of our imaginary frozen in time and immune to both critique and evidence so that the frozen artifact becomes the central religious tenet of the state. In the latter case, we are in real trouble. For then religion (secular or otherworldly) and the state are fused into a powerful doctrine that freezes the dynamic and dialectical development of culture.

So what do we make of the radical division between church and state that is such an integral mark of both the French and the American polities, but which manifest themselves in two opposite directions – banning religion from the political sphere in France and enhancing its role in politics in the United States? I only note that these are core elements in their political cultures but with no universal lessons. Canada has its own versions of state/church relations without raising neutrality onto an absolutist pedestal. Canada and Québec are, in practice, neutral with respect to religious institutions. The two polities are not neutral when it comes to traditions, whether they be Sunday and holiday closing laws or the preservation of symbols, even as they try to incorporate traditions of minorities. That is why it was correct for Premier Charest to reject the B-T recommendation and refuse to remove the cross above the Speaker's chair, since there was little indication in Québec practices that the state favoured Christianity in any significant way except to recognize that the Christian (and Catholic) religion was part of either the belief system or heritage of the vast majority of the province's population. The issue should not have been denial of this inheritance in the name of civic religion trumping an otherworldly religion. The issue at stake is only whether the state gives favour to one institution rather than to the others, or whether it discriminates among individuals based on religious affiliation.

In fact, Québécois demonstrate a marked schizophrenia to their Catholic past. Unlike the French, who act out their Catholic paternalism in their anti-clericalism, most Québécois secularists who have abandoned their Catholicism nevertheless embrace that Catholicism as an important part of their cultural heritage, even if it is only to differentiate their 'nation' from the ROC. Further, their loss of religion makes them cling to the singularity of their language in continental North America all the more tightly. That is also why they embrace a conception of 'thick' citizenship, rather than the 'thin' citizenship of the rest of Canada.

For the preservation of their language is an existential issue for the Québécois. And as immigration reduces their percentage of the population in Canada, and as immigrants are more attracted to English as a global language even more than its serving as the dominant language in Canada, and as francophones with global ambitions also must learn to master that language, the importance of preserving French does not diminish but becomes greater. Inevitably, there will be a tension between the need to preserve and enhance French and the need to respect the rights of individuals to make choices. However, for the survival of the French community, in this area communal values must trump individual choice.

Since multiculturalism is silent on language rights, and since Québec must give primacy to language rights and the preservation of the French culture as a small minority in a North American Anglo sea north of the Mexican border, interculturalism must trump multiculturalism in Québec – interculturalism entailing, on the one hand, greater restrictions on individual rights, and, on the other, a more expansive sense of respecting the traditions of a group. This does not make Québec francophone nationalism into an exclusionary cult that insists on homogeneity and continuity of a single group in space and in time. Quite the reverse! It can mean celebrating equality, justice, integration, and democracy, and celebrating change, mixing, and heterogeneity, but never at the cost of the core nation that constitutes Québec society. Individuals will continue to enjoy the whole panoply of freedoms and rights, of religious beliefs and practices, except when those threaten the existential life of the francophone nation. In Québec there will always be an admixture of ethnicity, nationalism, and laws protecting the continuity of the French language, but that nationalism need not be exclusionary.

Common Citizenship and Religious/Ethnic Diversity

That is also why, in Québec, and to a lesser degree in the ROC, religious diversity is respected and honoured, for everyone enjoys the same citizenship with the same rights and privileges. If an appreciation for diversity is the requisite of tolerance in a multicultural society, what are the requisites and benefits of a common citizenship? An appreciation of the richness of a multitude of cultures may enrich the imaginary muse and provide a rich historical seasoning to our lives in civil society, but are we not required to forge universal standards applicable to each and every citizen? No doubt. But covering the windows of a gymnasium in a Y with curtains or frosted glass to protect against the wayward but probing eye has nothing to add or subtract from the rights of all citizens. Almost all the issues that became contentious had nothing to do with the rights of citizens. They had to do with the rights of patrons or the right to expect equal service, or the rights to privacy or equal treatment *within civil society*. The reason, of course, is that citizens of Québec, as do citizens of the rest of Canada, already enjoy a very high level of protection of their common rights as citizens to be equal before the law. There is no suggestion in any of the controversies that the rights of citizens were under threat. The Canadian Charter of Rights and Freedoms does guarantee the rights and freedoms set out in that charter. Thus far, the Charter has not been subjected to limits considered reasonable as prescribed by law and *demonstrably justified* in a free and democratic society.

Clearly, common citizenship requires standards which spell out the rights, duties, and obligation of citizens and ensures their equality and autonomy. But these are not the positive values that will ensure that communities will both respect and appreciate differences and work out the compromises necessary to get on with life in the civil society. That requires an inculcation of values and norms by the common culture and not just by the state. Instead of simply relying on public schooling, as in France, to transfer a sense of public virtue, the whole culture must be involved and the enterprise viewed as one carried out through the life of the citizen. Further, that citizenship sense, which extends the concept into civil society, is not merely geared towards serving the national interests of the state, but directs its energies at ensuring that the local and the global environments cohere. It is an active concept of citizenship and not just a passive one, a concept of citizenship that is a matter of daily practice inculcating a respect for others and not just an assurance that individuals are treated with equal respect before the law. It is a conception of thick versus thin citizenship (Faulks 2000).

Thick versus Thin Citizenship: Forced Marriage and Radical Female Circumcision

In the cases documented in the Bouchard-Taylor Report, B-T made clear that freedom of the press and other media exacerbated the problems in the first place by inaccurate and exaggerated reporting. Yet not once did B-T suggest that freedom of the press be curtailed. Instead, implicitly B-T sought to educate the media about their failures and their responsibilities, not simply the fifth estate as a critic of government, but as an educator instead of an arouser of the public. However, all this occurred in a context in which the normative values implicit in the behaviour B-T endorsed were already part of the public fabric of Québec normative life. But let us take some cases where freedom of conscience, religion, and forms of belief and practice do conflict with Canadian and Québécois values.

There are numerous consensual arranged marriages between Canadian citizens and overseas brides and grooms. Sometimes immigration issues arise because there is a suspicion that such couplings are marriages of convenience to obtain Canadian citizenship. Otherwise, there is no incompatibility between Canadian values and consensual arranged marriages that allow the Canadian culture, emphasizing individual choice, to coexist alongside and intersect with more traditional cultures in which arranged marriages are the norm.

This is not true when, for example, a Pakistani parent sends his daughter back to Pakistan to be married to a man of the father's choice, and oftentimes against the expressed wishes of his daughter. These coerced or forced arranged marriages offend Canadian sensibilities and values, yet in a country like Somalia they still take place.[5] Canada noted that Canadian citizens, mainly women, were being forced into marriage in Somalia: '[P]arents, relatives and the community may use relentless pressure and emotional blackmail, threatening behaviour, abduction, imprisonment and physical violence to coerce young people to enter marriage.'[6]

There are many types of non-consensual arranged marriages: to marry a daughter who is approaching an age where men no longer wish to consider the woman as a bride, for example; or to seal a peace agreement between warring tribes as a result of a bribe to the father. Not one type is considered acceptable in terms of dominant Canadian values (May and Deepa 2007). Canada is opposed to forced marriages of any kind as a violation of international law to which Canada is a signatory.[7] Marriage may only be entered into with the full and free consent of the individual. Here, Canadian values and laws, reinforced by international law, are in direct opposition to communal practices. The Canadian government is active in efforts to prevent such marriages and rescue individuals forced to undergo such marriages. Just as Canadian values must trump and counter unacceptable values, multiculturalism and human rights should not be considered as labels upon which to defend exclusionary communities and practices that impose unacceptable restrictions on individuals.

Let us take a second case. In Canada the Criminal Code prohibits the genital mutilation or circumcision of females (usually the removal of outer parts of the clitoris, but in some cases involving more radical surgery), but not of males when their foreskins are removed. Female circumcision is a cultural practice and rite of passage that has been applied to well over a hundred million women; the failure to undergo circumcision is regarded by many women from those cultures as a matter of deep cultural humiliation – their social well-being, an integral component of health, could suffer. However, the Ontario College of Physicians and Surgeons has banned the practice, though an adult woman is free to undergo the procedure if her decision is voluntary and the woman understands the implications. No physician is forced to undertake the procedure. But physicians are obligated to refuse if the procedure is to be undertaken on a child not yet of the age of consent.

In both cases, Canadian cultural values as well as the law run counter to the cultural practice of a foreign community. Unequivocally, Canadian law and norms trump. But these are issues that affect the rights of the individual. Are there any such clashes that affect individuals in a public space, such as wearing a hijäb? In the one case, a Muslim judge ruled against the hijäb in a soccer match as a matter of safety, though it was treated as a matter of cultural discrimination when her teammates walked out of the tournament. However, this was a rare instance. Generally, inherited cultural practices are allowed to persist unless they are explicitly offensive. Minority cultural expressions are

Conclusion: Religion, Culture, and the State 113

tolerated unless some evidence is found to indicate otherwise. So why the brouhaha over reasonable accommodation?

Reasonable accommodation has an ordinary informal cultural, as well as a formal legal, meaning. That informal meaning provides the substance for Québec's intercultural version of multiculturalism. However, the issue is not just multiculturalism and a tolerance of one community for another, or even interculturalism and an active appreciation and respect for the other culture so that compromises can be worked out in a reasonable fashion in the day-to-day lives of ordinary people. Canadians want and need to articulate the values they hold as a common culture, values that take into account and preserve historical traditions as long as they do not reify the a priori rejection of cultural differences; and that take into consideration the needs of different regions of the country to manifest differences, including differences that utilize and preserve one language that is different than the one spoken in the rest of Canada. But those geographic conditions are not restricted to respecting and preserving linguistic differences, but recognizing that Albertans and those from Regina and Winnipeg may have different perspectives. British Columbians may be our foremost protectors of the environment, while Albertans may be foremost in protecting the strengths of individual enterprise. Thick citizenship allows for regional variation in response to and reflected in different sociopolitical structures and economic priorities to blossom.

The *Res Publica*: Xenophobic Political Opportunism versus Rational Debate

B-T, however, taught another lesson. There is a widespread conviction spread by philosophers, from Jürgen Habermas (1993) to Paul Ricoeur (1991, 1992) and from John Rawls (1997) to Charles Taylor (1985, 1994), that public disputes are best settled through public discourse in the marketplace of ideas. Hence the high value placed on public commissions and public hearings as populism is wedded to liberalism. However, in France the system was already skewed to reinforce the reification of laïcité. In Canada, the process gave voice to xenophobia and the maligning of other communities, though as Bina Freiwald's chapter illustrates, there were a significant number of articulate and well-thought-out briefs.

What is the foundation for the belief in the public sphere as a place of true rational debate and discourse as a mode of resolving socially contentious issues? It is one thing to adopt the conception of a res publica where any citizen can come forth to debate and discuss and hold in check state power. It is quite another to believe that very deeply *socially* divisive issues are best resolved by extending the parliamentary grounds for debate and discussion into civil society. There is no doubt that an arena of public debate now exists well outside the confines of the state. But to represent that debate in idealistic terms as the realm for rational debate and discourse is to be blind to how those who stimulate hate and suspicion use the same space to reify set attitudes and spread prejudice. To acknowledge that fact but blame it on the commercialization and development of a crass public media that treats citizens as simply consumers to be manipulated by their needs and wants is to misunderstand what is taking place. Or to blame the deterioration on the development of a state serving only competing interests is to engage in both naïve, idealistic idolatry of the eighteenth century and to miss the essential nature of mass twenty-first-century culture.

John Rawls (1997) believed such debate was a matter of advancing competing claims and modes of implementation in the public sphere, subjecting those claims to debate in order to resolve how primary social goods are distributed. The res publica, the idea of public reason as an essential sphere of a well-ordered constitutional democracy, offered means and the forum where conflicts get expressed and modes of negotiating a resolution are debated. The expectation was that good and enlightened judgment is the result of good deliberation and public debate. For in a pluralistic world that we want to ensure remains reasonable, there will be a plurality of conflicting religious, philosophical, and ethical norms that need to be mediated, while accepting that they cannot be reconciled. Rawls, however, unlike Habermas (1991) and Ricoeur (1991, 1992, with Canto-Serber 2004) restricted that debate to public officials (judges, senior mandarins, and legislators) and candidates for office, for it is the reason *of* the public that he was discussing. He also restricted the debate to constitutional issues and distributive justice about public goods. And they were about legislative enactments within a family of reasonable political conceptions of justice, all within an understanding of reciprocity.

However, B-T revealed that the issues in contention had nothing to do with distributive justice and were certainly not restricted to the views of public officials. Ironically, reciprocity seemed to be the guiding mark of conduct *before* the issue became a matter of public debate, and the issues were easily resolved if left to the good sense of the Québécois *within* civil society. Displaying them in the public sphere invited distortion and

Conclusion: Religion, Culture, and the State   115

brought forth irrationality. There was a huge gap between the ideal of public debate and its reality.

The central issue of process is how we avoid the perverted use of rhetoric, not only from the irrational elements in society, but also from the most rational, who are chained to their elitist doctrines of how the state *ought* to work, indifferent to the way it actually works? In fact, the latter are in a more entrenched position to manipulate public opinion than the so-called irrational forces. Rawls' proposed forum of public debate that set restrictions on what reasons could be proffered in the public debate was irrelevant.

One can fall back on the comforting position that although public discourse is extremely fragile, there is no better alternative if we are to understand how we operate as political animals in the public sphere. But then why was mutual respect so much in evidence in the private sphere and civil society before the spotlight was put on the event to distort those situations and give rise to so much public disrespect? And why was mutual *dis*respect so much in evidence when brought out into the clear light of day? The answer that there is nothing better to offer to replace the res publica is a cop-out, especially when these issues are so existentially central when ethnic nationalist mobilization is being engineered, either in transitions to independence from collectivist authoritarian societies to liberal ones (Meadwell 1993). The debate cannot be restricted, neither in its content nor to certain participants. However, the forum can be controlled so that the media are not used to provide a platform for insulting and demeaning other cultures.

B-T was dubbed Québec's truth and reconciliation commission. B-T was about truth in the most fundamental empirical sense about what happened, when, and why, and this methodology contrasted with the Stasi Commission. However, it did not appear to be about reconciliation. It was a political distraction for political purposes and the process made things worse as the subsequent polls indicated; the hearings sewed dissension rather than reconciliation. However, the B-T Commission had the benefit of establishing that rights are historically rooted and have to be interpreted within an historical context. Further, the brilliance of the Report was that it was fundamentally based on reconciliation. For instead of viewing individualism and communitarianism as polar opposites subject to an either/or logic, Taylor and Bouchard treated them as reconcilable principles. Individualism was but the vertical axis and communitarianism the horizontal axis in a sine graph. The authors employed 'both/and' rather than 'either/or' logic. They brought clarity to the debate, and for that alone the results should be celebrated.

Theory and Practice: Concrete Practices and Theoretical Postulates

The greatest benefit that B-T provided was the empirical revelation that these issues were being handled with little fuss and great aplomb by ordinary citizens with great practical wisdom. People do and must belong to a society. But those societies are not static. They are living organisms subjected to a continuous interaction of competing moral and cultural forces. Human beings in ordinary situations are very capable of using their imagination and intelligence to cross cultural divides in concrete situations. What the report also seemed to establish is that liberation from past irrationality can only be accomplished through enhancing and strengthening the rationality of a society in its behaviour and practices. A rational public world of debate to resolve these problems in civil society is an illusion. This enlightened area of the res publica, rather than reaffirming and reinforcing the possibility of individuals pursuing their own ends in freedom, both individually and socially, can and generally does become a forum for the intolerant and the xenophobic rather than being used for reciprocal rational discourse. Opportunities for rational discourse are applicable where the issues are not tolerance and respect but getting on in the world. Reciprocity is best learned when people share tasks, not when they engage in abstract debates about fundamentals. By the time these debates are long forgotten, their children will be enjoying their mutually altered world together. Allow the Scottish common sense of David Hume and Adam Smith to play itself out, and be very wary of looking to sweet reason to resolve such issues.

Notes

Introduction

1 The initial discussions around this theme were held by the authors of this book at the 12th Biennial Jerusalem Conference in Canadian Studies held at the Hebrew Centre for Canadian Studies in June 2008, under the auspices of the Halbert Centre for Canadian Studies.
2 Following Québec's language law, the Commission was given an official name in French only. In the English version, the designation is 'The Consultation Commission on Accommodation Practices Related to Cultural Differences in Response to Public Discontent Concerning Reasonable Accommodation,' which is somewhat different from the French title. A complete report (310 pp.) and an abridged report (99 pp.) are available in an English translation on the Commission's website [last accessed June 2009] at http://www.accommodements.qc.ca/index-en.html.
3 Gérard Bouchard is a professor in the Department of Human Sciences at the University of Québec at Chicoutimi. He holds a master's degree in sociology from Laval University (1968) and a PhD in history from the University of Paris (1971). He is the director and founder of the BALSAC Project, created in 1972, which has developed a computerized population database covering the population of Québec from the seventeenth century to the present that facilitates scientific research projects in many areas, including history and sociology, population genetics, and genetic epidemiology. Prof. Bouchard was also director and founder of the SOREP Centre, launched in 1977, which was transformed in 1994 into IREP, an inter-university institute for population research involving seven Québec universities. Under his direction for the first four years, the Institute developed into an international institution made up of 50 researchers and more than 2,750 professionals,

assistants, and technicians. Over the past several years, Prof. Bouchard initiated a new research program on the comparative history of new societies or founding cultures to study the formation of nations and cultures in the New World (the Americas, Australasia, some parts of Africa); to explore
national myths, political emancipation, collective differentiation from the European mother countries, the growth of the state and of the national idea, the formation of collective imaginaries (identity, memory, utopia), and the evolution of the relationship with Aboriginal peoples. In February 2002, Prof. Bouchard became the holder of a Canada Research Chair in the Comparative Dynamics of Collective Imaginaries. Prof. Bouchard has authored, co-authored, edited, or co-edited 36 books, and has published 268 papers in scientific journals. His most recent books include the novel *Mistouk* (2002); *Raison et contradiction: Le mythe au secours de la pensée* (2003); *Les deux chanoines: Contradiction et ambivalence dans la pensée de Lionel Groulx* (2003); *La pensée impuissante. Échecs et mythes nationaux canadiens-français, 1850–1960* (2004); the novel *Pikauba* (2005); *La culture québécoise est-elle en crise?* (with Alain Roy) (2007); *Mythes et sociétés des Amériques* (edited with Bernard Andrès) (2007); *The Making of the Nations and Cultures of the New World: An Essay in Comparative History* (Trans. of *Genèse des nations et cultures du Nouveau Monde: Essai d'histoire comparée*, 2000) (2008). With Charles Taylor, he co-authored *Building the Future: A Time for Reconciliation* (report of the Consultation Commission on Accommodation Practices Related to Cultural Differences) (2008). Finally, he published the novel *Uashat* (2009).

4 Born in 1931 in Montréal, Charles Taylor is a Canadian philosopher and political theorist, who, as a Rhodes scholar at Balliol College, earned his PhD under the supervision of Isaiah Berlin and G.E.M. Anscombe. Except for his return to Oxford in 1976 as the Chichele professor of political and social theory at All Souls College, a position he held for six years, he has been a professor of political science and philosophy in the Department of Political Science at McGill University until his retirement. Subsequently he took up a position in the Department of Philosophy and the School of Law at Northwestern University in Evanston, Illinois. His initial writings focused on methodology and the philosophy of the social sciences; he offered a critique of behaviourism in his doctoral thesis, which was published as *The Explanation of Behaviour* (1964). In that book, he argued that the social sciences were more akin to an interpretive than a natural science. The next year, he ran for federal Parliament (he had previously run in 1962 and 1963) against Pierre Trudeau, who won and subsequently

became Prime Minister of Canada. He published *Pattern of Politics* (1970). He subsequently wrote *Hegel* (1975) and *Hegel and Modern Society* (1979), and his papers were collected in a two-volume set, *Philosophical Papers* (1985). He has since published *Sources of the Self: The Making of Modern Identity* (1989); his Massey Lectures, published as *The Malaise of Modernity* (1991); *Reconciling the Solitudes: Essays on Canadian Federalism and Nationalism* (1993); *Multiculturalism: Examining the Politics of Recognition* (1994); *A Catholic Modernity* (1999); *Varieties of Religion Today: William James Revisited* (2002); and *Modern Social Imaginaries* (2004). In 2007, he won the Templeton Prize (which included a cash award of US$1.5 million) for Progress toward Research or Discoveries about Spiritual Realities. His book, *The Secular Age* (2007), also won the *Publishers Weekly* Best Book (2007), the Christianity Today Book Award for History/Biography (2008), a *Globe and Mail* Best Book of the Year (2008), a *Tablet* Best Book of the Year (2008); the Henry Paolucci/Walter Bagehot Book Award (2008), the *New York Times* Notable Book of 2008, and a *Times Literary Supplement* Book of the Year (2008). Charles Taylor also won the 2008 Kyoto Prize in Arts and Philosophy (the Japanese Nobel) given by the Inamori Foundation, and was himself the subject of two collections of essays: *Philosophy in an Age of Pluralism: The Philosophy of Charles Taylor in Question*, edited by James Tully and Daniel M. Weinstock (Cambridge University Press, 1995); and *Charles Taylor*, edited by Ruth Abbey (Cambridge University Press, 2004). Charles Taylor has also been actively involved in Canadian politics. He was vice-president of the federal New Democratic Party (NDP) and president of the Québec NDP. Charles Taylor is a Companion of the

Order of Canada. With Gerard Bouchard, he co-authored *Building the Future: A Time for Reconciliation* (Report of the Consultation Commission on Accommodation Practices Related to Cultural Differences) (Québec Government, 2008).
5 Cited from the Canadian Multicultural Act, R.S. 1985, c. 24 (4th Supp.) 3 (1) (c).
6 Cited from 'Québec interculturel,' ministère de l'Immigration et des Communautés culturelles, gouvernement du Québec. www.Quebecinterculturel.gouv.qc.ca/valeurs-fondements/index.html [accessed February 2010]. Translation provided by the author.
7 Gopnik 2009b: 30. In contrast to other views of cosmopolitanism that insist that individuals do and *should* be able to move between and among particular cultures without any hindrance or state-supported inhibitions, the Canadian-rooted variety advocate state support to enable minority cultural membership to be preserved.
8 See note 2 above.

1: Reasonable Accommodation in the Canadian Legal Context

1 Canadian Multiculturalism Act, Law C-31, 1988, Article 3, Section 1a, Department of Justice Canada. www.solon.org/Statutes/Canada/English/C/CMA [accessed February 2010].
2 Ibid. Article 3, Section 1d.
3 Canadian Multiculturalism, in Parliamentary Information and Research Service, Library of Parliament (2006: 11). www.parl.gc.ca/information/library/PRBpubs/936-e.htm#acanadian [accessed February 2010].
4 These interpretations by Aboriginal traditionalists do not supersede the fundamental rights contained in the Charter, and known under Sections 7 to 9 as the right to life, liberty, and security of person. It would be acceptable, though, for a Canadian citizen, under the fundamental freedoms provided by Article 2, to reject the *concept* of human rights itself, providing that this remains an opinion which does not seek to negate the fundamental rights of other individuals.
5 These numbers were taken from the report of the Consultation Commission on Accommodation Practices Related to Cultural Differences, better known as the Bouchard-Taylor Commission (Montreal, 2008).
6 Despite its Anglo-Protestant name dating back to another era, the YMCA (Young Men's Christian Association) on Avenue du Parc is open to people of all backgrounds and religions. In this case, negotiations dealt with the relevance of installing curtains, blinds, or frosted glass in the windows of the building in order to prevent someone outside or next door (young Satmar boys) from seeing the female clientele working out in the gym.
7 See the mandate of the Commission as described at www.accommodements.qc.ca/commission/mandat.html [accessed February 2010].
8 Ibid.
9 The report of the Commission is available at www.accommodements.qc.ca/commission/mandat.html [accessed March 2009; February 2010] in its complete version (310 pp.) and in its abridged version (101 pp.) This quotation is taken from an excerpt published in *Le Devoir* (23 May 2008: A-9) under the title 'Le temps de la conciliation.'
10 *Le Devoir* (23 May 2008): A-9.
11 Ibid.
12 See the recommendations of the Commission as described at www.accommodements.qc.ca/commission/mandat.html [accessed March 2009; February 2010].

2: Monoculturalism versus Interculturalism in a Multicultural World

1 Hijāb derives from the Arabic word for 'barrier' or 'veil,' and its primary reference is to the curtain that separates men and women in prayer. However, we know the term in reference to a type of kerchief and not a veil, though, revealingly, the debate in France focused on the *le voule* (veil) when referring explicitly to the hijāb (Zouari 2002, 2004). In France *foulard*, though it just means scarf, has come to be associated with the hijāb, and *écharpe* is now used to refer to a non-Muslim headscarf (see Allen 2008).
2 In a parliamentary address on 22 June 2009, President Sarkozy of France announced that the burqa was 'not welcome' in France. On 5 April 2010 the Québec government introduced a bill to ban wearing the niqab when an individual asked for services from a public agency or when working for the government, after a controversy had arisen when a Muslim woman wearing a niqab was expelled from her French language course after five weeks because she would not take off the niqab as a condition for attending the course.
3 These include Tunisia and Turkey, both Muslim countries.
4 This was the theme for the Nordic Migration Research Conference on international migration and ethnic relations research in Bergen, Norway, 14–16 November 2007; an early version of this paper was first presented there.
5 Thomas Deltombe (2005) describes an imaginary Islam that French politicians use to define a new political consensus and assert a conservative conception of national identity. Modood (2005) argues that whereas France integrates individuals who may happen to be Muslim, Britain integrates Islam as a single community.
6 'Veiling' has a complex and long history. Many Muslim women cover themselves as an affirmation of cultural identification with a rich and varied tradition. For others, wearing a headdress or veil is a modern feminist statement. In some contexts, the veil clearly marginalizes women in society. In others, a headscarf de-marginalizes and expresses liberation from colonial legacies. To preserve their sexual identity, some women wear a headscarf to avert the male gaze. Others do so as a sign of rank and nuanced social status. What women wear on their heads and bodies is always intimately connected with notions of the self, the body, the community, and the cultural construction of identity, privacy, and space (El Guindi 1999). Contemporary veiling can be about piety or self-expression, or can make a social statement about resistance and preservation, privacy, and public identity (Mahmood 2005).
7 Cf. Bernard-Patel (2008) for a comparison of France with Britain.

8 Cf. Weil (2009), who offers figures of 2.21 per cent for Protestants and 0.2 per cent for Jews. According to the *Concise Britannica Online Encyclopedia*, of a 41.9 million French population in 1900, approximately 500,000, or 12 per cent, were Protestant, whereas, according to vol. I of the *American Jewish Yearbook*, there were 72,000 Jews; however, Zeza Szajkowski (1946), in *The Growth of the Jewish Population in France: The Political Aspects of Demographic Politics*, provides a figure of 86,885 Jews in France.
9 Avis du Conseil d'Etat, 27 November 1989, No. 346893. http://www.conseiletat.fr/ce/missio/index_mi_cg03_01.shtml.
10 '[T]he wearing by students, in the schools, of signs whereby they believe to be manifesting their adherence to one religion is itself not incompatible with the principle of laïcité, since it constitutes the exercise of their liberty of expression and manifestation of their religious beliefs; but this liberty does not permit students to exhibit [*d'arborer*] signs of religious belonging which, by their nature, by the conditions under which they are worn individually and collectively, or by their ostentatious or combative [*revendicatif*] character, would constitute an act of pressure, provocation, proselytizing or propaganda, threatening to the dignity or liberty of the student or to the other members of the educational community, compromising their health or their security, disturbing the continuation of institutional activities or the educational role of the instructors, in short, [that] would disturb proper order in the establishment or the normal functioning of public service' (Weil 2009: 2701).
11 There are debates over the actual numbers, some estimating the real figure to be five or even 10 times the official figures (Cf. Weil 2009: 2707; Renault and Touraine 2005: 79).
12 Translated by Lucy R. McNair and published in English as *To Hell and Back: The Life of Samira Bellil* (Lincoln: University of Nebraska Press, 2008).
13 This growing belief was supported by sensational cases in other jurisdictions that were widely reported. For example, in New South Wales in a suburb of Sydney, Australia, in August 2000, eight Muslim youths tracked down Australian girls, whom they called 'Aussie pigs,' and forced two teenage girls to perform oral sex on them; two days later, two of the men raped a 16-year-old girl. At the end of the month, the gang grew to 14, and repeatedly raped another teenage girl. The members of the gang received sentences of 11- to 55-year terms, much longer than the eight-year sentences the rapists of Samira Bellil received from the French courts.
14 Djavann had a strong impact on the veil debate in France, including on the discussions that took place in the French parliament prior to the passing of the 2004 law banning the hijāb. She stressed over and over again that Islam

can exist without the veil, but the Islamist system cannot, because 'the veil is the symbol, the flag and the keystone of the Islamic system,' for Islamism only sees women's heads as genitalia. Dévoilez Chahdorff (2003). This was also cited in her interview with Isabelle Robineau in the French literary monthly *Topo*. http://66 249 93. 104/search?q=cache:llTZshokp qwJ:www.chapitre.com/accueil.asp%3.

15 The report of the commission was published on 11 December 2003. The 70-page report was divided into four sections (http://www.communau tarisme.net/commissionstas):
   1. History and philosophical principles of secularism
   2. Legal principles
   3. Contemporary challenges
   4. Framing and recommendations

   For public submissions, see http://lesrapports.ladocumentationfrancaise .fr/BRP/034000725/0000.pdf.

16 The law in France has a fundamental unifying baseline of la laïcité. Contrast that with debates over legal pluralism in other jurisdictions. Though there are many conceptions of legal pluralism (Dupret 2007), there are some common fundamental premises concerning the nature of law, its function, and its relationship with its cultural milieu. In this context, in contrast to France's unitary system of civic law, Québec mixes its civil law tradition with the common-law tradition that is the foundation of law in Canada. However, our stress is not primarily on how the legal tradition(s) specifically influence policies in handling diversity, but on the political culture within which the system of law plays a part.

17 *See* http://sisyphe.org/article.php3?id_ARTICLE+677.

18 In France, wearing the hijāb in schools or when accessing or providing government services is viewed as a threat to the domestic secular republican order, la laïcité (Renaut and Touraine 2005) – the widely shared faith in French republicanism and secularism, as well as the basic law of France for defining citizenship. In spite of historic and ethnic differences among its citizens, in the strong version of laïcité, France upholds a set of common values as the foundation for a single and undivided republic based on the rights of the individual and individual conscience, the separation of church and state, and the neutrality of the state towards all religions epitomized by the phrase, 'all citizens are equal.' In the doctrine of laïcité, religious and ethnic differences are bracketed in the public realm (Baubérot 2000; Pena-Ruiz 2005; Barnett and Duvall 2005). 'If you support secularity, you support liberty; that is, freedom from the disciplines and shackles of religion ... you support maintaining a distance between all spiritual or

community affiliation in the public arena, thus making all equal and the same in civil life. If you stand for secularity, you stand for the construction of a space for citizens where all men, and especially all women, can be united, whatever their belief or their faith' (Levy 2004).
19 Laborde is only a qualified defender, for she justifies the action but on different grounds. In her book *Critical Republicanism: The Hijāb Controversy and Political Philosophy* (2008), in the first section, she sets out a republican perfectionist case for the ban on the hijāb based on enlightenment assumptions about progressive secular rationalism, education for individual autonomy, and criticism of the pre-modern, patriarchal nature of Islam, the same way Catholicism was critiqued. Laborde then takes up the position of the criticisms of this ban that rejects republican paternalism. In the third section, Laborde argues that both the justification and the criticism are flawed, for although the ban on the hijāb cannot be justified on liberal premises, the fear driving republicans is correct. So Laborde purports to offer a 'critical republican' theory which eschews communal paternalism and the domination and repression that entails by basing her theory on empowering the individual.
20 The new legislation was signed into law by then president Jacques Chirac on 15 March 2004 as Law 2004-228. The law came into effect at the beginning of the new school year on 2 September 2004. The full title of the law is *Loi n° 2004-228 du 15 mars 2004 encadrant, en application du principe de laïcité, le port de signes ou de tenues manifestant une appartenance religieuse dans les écoles, collèges et lycées publics.*
21 *Le Figaro* (6 November 2004); *Libération* (10 November 2004).
22 21 January 2004 survey for *Le Parisien.*
23 'Cité des 4000,' la Courneuve; 'La Madeleine,' Evreux; 'Val Fourré,' Mantes la Jolie; 'Les Minguettes,' Vénissieux, near Lyon. Roy (2005) argues that these suburban youth are uprooted in every sense of the term. They are disenfranchised youth, people who have lost their way, who don't know who they are. In the Parisian suburbs, both Islamic and evangelical preaching have increased, both very much resented by the local authorities. According to Roy, this individualism and alienation is reinforced in France by the shift from the concept of cultural minorities to the concept of faith communities based on personal, individual choice, a choice he endorses while disparaging the consequences.
24 ADQ won 41 seats. In the December 2008 elections they were reduced to seven seats and Mario Dumont resigned.
25 Cf. Hugh Winsor (2007). 'Québec's Le Pen likely to make major electoral gain,' *The Independent* (26 March). http://www.independent.co.uk/news/

world/americas/Québecs-le-pen-likely-to-make-major-election-gain-441867.html.
26 The Ontario and Québec soccer associations in Canada differed on whether headscarves should be permitted or banned when girls played soccer. Québec soccer referees ejected an 11-year-old girl from Laval, Québec, for refusing to take off her headscarf when playing in a soccer tournament. When Asmahan Mansour, a player for the Nepean U12 Hotspurs, was ejected by a Muslim referee, the Ontario team walked out in protest, contending that as long as the headscarf was safely tucked in and secured, it posed no hazard. Just two weeks after he set up a provincial commission to investigate the issue of 'reasonable accommodation' with respect to the toleration of differences, Jean Charest, Québec's premier, weighed into the debate defending the Québec referee's ban, insisting that the referee was just enforcing safety rules. The issue is not simply about what divides Canada from France, but what divides France from Québec, and Québec from Ontario and the rest of Canada.
27 Rachad (2008), in analysing the coverage of 'reasonable accommodation' in Québec newspapers (four francophones and one anglophone), via both text analysis software and a grid analysis, concluded that the images and the words ('irrationality,' 'hatred') for portraying the debate in 2007 were not drawn from local contexts but from an international one, thereby partially explaining the distortions, and how minor issues were transformed into crises.
28 The term 'multicultural' has a variety of meanings, but is generally used to describe a religiously and culturally diverse society. It also depicts the prescriptive norms for managing that diversity while sometimes contributing to exacerbating its internal tensions. In Canada, it generally means not only accommodating but encouraging that diversity. In contrast, the British model simply tolerates and recognizes that diversity. Cf. Tariq Modood (2008), who argues that the British (in contrast to the French), rather than reifying a traditional identity, have engaged in what Modood calls 'civic re-balancing' arising out of a principle of racial equality of the 1965 Race Relations Act that recognizes difference while promoting equality of access and opportunity. See also May, Modood, and Squires (2004) and Modood (2000).

3: The Bouchard-Taylor Commission and the Jewish Community of Quebec in Historical Perspective

1 Pierre Anctil, 'Quel accommodement raisonnable?' *Le Devoir* (11 December 2006). http://www.ledevoir.com/2006/12/11/124575.html [accessed 16 May 2008].

2 Québec political observer Lysiane Gagnon blamed a portion of the Québec media for fanning the flames of the controversy. Cited in Martin C. Barry (*The Chronicle*, 11 December 2007). A journalistic account of the Commission has appeared in book form: Heinrich and Dufour (2008).
3 It should be noted that issues similar in nature to those driving the debate on 'reasonable accommodation' in Québec were also quite influential in the Ontario provincial election in the fall of 2007, namely public funding of faith-based schools other than Catholic, as well as concerning the relation of Muslim Sharia law and the Ontario Arbitration Act. *See* Chris Cobb, 'Most Canadians want limits on accommodating minorities, poll finds,' CanWest News Service (25 September 2007). www.cjc.ca/template.php?action=ioi&item=153 [accessed 18 March 2008]; Gerald Gall, 'Religious accommodation,' *Canadian Jewish News* (3 January 2008). For an example of how the hearings have influenced discussion on similar issues elsewhere in Canada, see 'Unreasonable accommodation' [editorial], *National Post* (19 October 2007), A12.
4 Mark Abley, 'An airing of old-stock grievances,' *The Star* (9 October 2007). www.thestar.com/printArticle/264800 [accessed 19 March 2008].
5 B'nai Brith Brief, October 2007. Cf. Alison Haynes, 'A Social Debate: Jewish groups say caricatures "in less than good taste,"' *National Post* (28 June 2007). www.vigile.net/Québec-cartoons-hit-ethnicity [accessed 18 March 2008].
6 Jim Coggins, canadianchristianity.com [accessed 18 March 2008].
7 *The Globe and Mail* (11 September 2007).
8 Lynne Cohen, *Jewish Tribune* (Toronto) (17 April 2008), 12. This allegation was challenged by the Commission's representative, Sylvain Leclerc, and defended by B'nai Brith. *See* Janice Arnold, 'B'nai Brith differs with accommodation commission,' *Canadian Jewish News* (8 May 2008), 3, 20.
9 David Lazarus, 'Fear of Islam fuels accommodation debate, Trudeau says,' *Canadian Jewish News* (20 December 2007), 6.
10 Jeff Heinrich, 'Do not fear Muslims,' Canwest News Service (17 May 2008).
11 Garth Stevenson (2008), review of Xavier Gélinas, *La droite intellectuelle Québécoise et la Revolution tranquille, American Historical Review* 113 (April), 486.
12 The Commission's analysis of all its hearings found that 'five per cent of the comments expressed could be characterized as "harsh," while another 12 to 15 per cent were "borderline offensive."' Janice Arnold, 'B'nai Brith differs with accommodation commission,' *Canadian Jewish News* (8 May 2008). www.CanadianJewishNews.com/index2.php?option=com_content&task.
13 Elias Levy, 'Un débat sur l'avenir de la société québécoise,' *Canadian Jewish News* (20 December 2007). The disquiet felt in English Canada is expressed in the title of an article appearing in *Maclean's* magazine of 22 October 2007,

by Martin Patriquin: 'Canada: A nation of bigots?' http://www.macleans.ca/canada/features/article.jsp?content=20071022_110249_110249&page=2 [accessed 14 May 2008].
14 Stevenson, review of Xavier Gélinas. See note 11 above.
15 Cited in Howard Bokser, 'Becoming unreasonable,' *Concordia University Magazine* (winter 2007/08), 3.
16 Québec political observer Lysiane Gagnon cited in Martin C. Barry, 'Québec columnist fingers tabloid for fanning fire in "accommodation" debate,' *The Chronicle* (11 December 2007). www.westendchronicle.com/article-166574 [accessed 19 March 2008].
17 Elias Levy, 'Un débat sur l'avenir de la société québécoise,' *Canadian Jewish News* (20 December 2007).
18 *National Post* (19 October 2007), A1, 9.
19 Graeme Hamilton, 'Giving gender equality priority called dangerous.' *National Post* (11 October 2007), A6.
20 Justin Trudeau, in a speech at a Montreal synagogue, charged that, in essence, the issue was 'prejudice against Muslims.' David Lazarus, *Canadian Jewish News* (20 December 2007).
21 Sheldon Gordon, 'Québec Jews Rethinking Traditional Ties to Province's Liberal Party.' *Forward* (20 June 2007). www.forward.com/articles/11002/ [accessed 18 March 2008].
22 David Lazarus, 'Québecers' view of Jews sets them apart, poll finds,' *Canadian Jewish News* (28 February 2008), 3.
23 'Kosher Tax.' http://en.wikipedia.org/wiki/Kosher_tax [accessed 18 May 2008].
24 These accusations were ultimately denounced by Gérard Bouchard as anti-Semitic. Caroline Touzin and Laura-Julie Perreault, 'Bouchard-Taylor: mythes et réalités,' *La Presse* (26 November 2007). www.cyberpresse.ca/apps/pbcs.dll/article?AID/20071126/ [accessed 19 March 2007]; Janice Arnold, 'Chassidim dismiss complaints against them at hearings,' *Canadian Jewish News* (6 December 2007), 3; (20 December 2007), 3.
25 Philip Authier and Mike De Souza, 'Charest bristles at criticism of fund hike for Jewish schools,' *The Gazette* (19 February 2005). http://www.vigile.net/Charest-bristles-at-criticism-of [accessed 18 May 2008]; Cf. Waller (2006). http://www.ajcarchives.org/AJC_DATA/Files/AJYB607.CV.pdf [accessed 18 May 2008]; Janice Arnold, 'CJC defends public funding of Jewish schools at hearings,' *Canadian Jewish News* (20 December 2007), 3.
26 Graeme Hamilton, 'Losing faith in Québec,' *National Post* (3 November 2007). http://www.nationalpost.com/news/story.html?id=08876ab3-a800-4995-b9d0-7eea7a703938&k=60734&p=1 [accessed 18 May 2008].

27 Jeff Heinrich, *The Gazette* (24 September 2007).
28 'Faces of the Year: the Accommodation Debate,' *The Gazette* (27 December 2007), A4. http://enmasse.ca/forums/viewtopic.php?t=5615.
29 Janice Arnold, *Canadian Jewish News* (6 December 2007), 3.
30 Jeff Heinrich, 'Hasidim anger residents,' *The Gazette* (26 September 2007).
31 The issue of kosher food at Montreal's Jewish General Hospital was in the news in early 2007 when the Québec Human Rights Commission ordered the Hospital to pay $10,000 to an ambulance driver who brought non-kosher food into the kosher cafeteria and was ordered out after refusing to leave. The commission ruled that the hospital failed to provide reasonable accommodation in that case. 'Montreal Jewish Hospital fined for enforcing kosher rules.' http://magicstatistics.com/2007/02/06 [accessed 19 March 2008].
32 Liz Ferguson, 'A one-year chronology of the province's "reasonable accommodation" controversy. *The Gazette* (3 February 2007). http://www.canada.com/montrealgazette/news/montreal/story.html?id=9abb439c-b103-4ee5-816b-a35c61ad4bfd&k=71765 [accessed 18 May 2008]; Chaim Steinmetz (2007) 'Reasonable Accommodation, Reasonable People' (13 December). http://chaimsteinmetz.blogspot.com/2007/02/reasonable-accommodation-reasonable.html [accessed 19 March 2008].
33 Zosia Bielski, 'Ban teachers from religious dress, women's group says.' *National Post* (9 October 2007), A1; Janice Arnold, *Canadian Jewish News* (20 December 2007).
34 Janice Arnold, *Canadian Jewish News* (22 November 2007), 3.
35 Janice Arnold, *Canadian Jewish News* (6 December 2007), 3.
36 One presenter in St Jerome stated that 'Les juifs sont le tremplin de l'argent national.' Stéphane Baillargeon, 'La commission Bouchard Taylor s'arrête à Saint-Jérôme. Les plus vieux se défoulent,' *Le Devoir* (25 September 2007). http://www.ledevoir.com/2007/09/25/158183.html [accessed 16 May 2008]. This was slightly mistranslated in the anglophone press as: 'Jews are ... the most powerful ... the trampoline of money in the world.' Jeff Heinrich, *The Gazette* (24 September 2007).
37 'The Future of Reasonable Accommodation,' *The Gazette* (15 December 2007). www.cjc.ca/template.php?action=oped&Rec=217.
38 'Care For All: A Brief to the Consultation Commission on Accommodation Practices Related to Cultural Differences,' October 2007, 1.
39 http://bnaibrith.ca/files/brief-final-eng.pdf [accessed 19 May 2008], 3–4.
40 Ibid., 6, 8.
41 Janice Arnold, *Canadian Jewish News* (21 February 2008).
42 Chaim Steinmetz, http://chaimsteinmetz.blogspot.com/ (13 February 2007).

43 '2006 Audit of Antisemitic Incidents,' http://www.bnaibrith.ca /au dit2006-D.html [accessed 18 March 2008].
44 Leaked copies of the report were circulated shortly before that, and generated press coverage. Jeff Heinrich, 'Findings Hailed as Road Map for Integration,' *The Gazette* (17 May 2008). http://www.canada.com:80/ montrealgazette/news/story.html?id=e4bdfdff-bfe5-4356-a408-16ed f6e9f652 [accessed 19 May 2008].
45 Janice Arnold, 'Québec should fight anti-Semitism, Bouchard-Taylor report says.' *Canadian Jewish News* (29 May 2008), 1, 22.
46 'Canadian Jewish Congress, Québec Region, congratulates Professors Gérard Bouchard and Charles Taylor,' Canadian Jewish Congress, Québec Region News Release (23 May 2008).
47 Janice Arnold, 'Community has mixed reaction to report,' *Canadian Jewish News* (Montreal edition)(29 May 2008), 22.
48 Pierre Anctil's 1988 relatively optimistic account of this encounter was corrected by Delisle (1993). Delisle's criticism of Québec anti-Semitism led to a lengthy and serious debate within French Canadian intellectual circles on the nature of Québec's historical relationship with its Jewish community.
49 For an interesting early twentieth century document relevant to the banning of *shehita*, see Ira Robinson (1985): 143–5.
50 For an example of a kosher certification agency's take on this issue, see http://www.ok.org/Content.asp?ID=76 [accessed July 18, 2008].
51 See note 38 above.
52 Henry Aubin, 'The brain drain of anglos from Québec is getting serious,' *The Gazette* (6 March 2008), A19.
53 Jeff Heinrich, 'Findings Hailed as Road Map for Integration.' *The Gazette* (Saturday, 17 May 2008). faisalkutty.com/.../findings-hailed-as-road-map for-integration-lines-of-communication-were-opened-one-member-of-advisory-panel-notes/.

4: 'Qui est nous?' Some Answers from the Bouchard-Taylor Commission's Archive

1 'Le présent débat m'interpelle personnellement au niveau de notre entité comme collectivité' (Godin 2007: 2). Throughout this chapter, the translations from French into English of cited passages from the briefs ('mémoires') presented to the Bouchard-Taylor Commission are mine. I have provided the original passages in these notes.

I would like to acknowledge with gratitude the help of the research assistant on this project, Catherine Dan-Vi Le-Huynh, and the support from a Concordia Faculty Development Grant.

2 Sunera Thobani has identified similar pitfalls in the Canadian state's focus on multiculturalism: 'It has reified culture as the most salient factor in intergroup dynamics, deflecting attention from the disquieting legacy of white supremacy and casting people of color as culturally problematic' (Thobani 2007: 162).

3 I look at some of the ways in which 'I' and 'we' are conjugated in political and personal narratives in Québec in Freiwald (2002).

4 'Le drame consiste dans le fait que les chartes québécoises et canadiennes ne reconnaissent à toutes fins pratiques que les droits individuels. C'est là une erreur à corriger ... Nos droits collectifs donc doivent être considérés' (Gros-Louis 2007: 3).

5 'Chaque être humain cherche normalement une réponse à cette question: qui suis-je dans la collectivité ambiante? La collectivité se pose aussi la même question. Qui sommes-nous comme collectivité québécoise?' (Godin 2007: 3).

6 'héritage,' 'sa culture ... ses traditions' (Godin 2007, 8).

7 'Cet héritage *contient aussi* des valeurs fondatrices nous semblant non négociables comme l'égalité entre les personnes indépendamment de la race, de la religion et de la nature de l'ethnie, la démocratie et la liberté d'expression et de religion' (Godin 2007: 8; emphasis added).

8 'Pour un nouvel équilibre entre tous les 'Nous' Québécois.'

9 'Il faut commencer par rétablir les repères majoritaires. Que sont-ils? Démocratie, égalité des sexes, charte des droits, liberté de religion? C'est bon, on a compris ! On vient d'égrener le dénominateur commun de toutes les sociétés démocratiques. Non. Je parle de la différence québécoise. À grands traits: le Québec existe parce que sa majorité a vécu une histoire singulière, parle le français et est porteuse d'une tradition religieuse. Les évacuer, les dévaluer, c'est perdre son estime de soi et, à terme, détester l'autre' (Lisée 2007: 3).

10 'La minorité d'hier est devenue la majorité d'aujourd'hui et elle craint que les nouveaux arrivants ne leur imposent une autre façon d'être, d'autres valeurs ou contre-valeurs. Nous sommes le plus bel exemple de ce qui pourrait lui arriver' (Gros-Louis 2007: 5).

11 'un héritage comme la langue, la religion et une culture sociale' (Godin 2007: 4).

12 'Je fais partie du peuple fondateur de ce pays. Environ 800 ancêtres du coté paternel et autant du coté maternel. Onze générations de Bisson, de Tardif, de Pinard, de Bourassa, de Fréchette ... etc.' (Bisson 2007: 3).

13 'On peut dire de moi que je suis un Québécois de souche. Selon mes notes généalogiques, mes ancêtres seraient arrivés tôt pendant le temps du Régime français. Au musée Pointe-à-Callière, à Montréal, on peut lire, sur une pierre, que là est le lieu ou un dénommé Jacques Archambault aurait, en 1658 sur ordre du gouverneur, creusé le premier puits à Montréal. Cet Archambault serait l'ancêtre de tous les Archambault. J'en suis' (Paiement 2007: 1).

14 'un orphelin abusé' (Émery 2007: 4); 'je me sens déraciné d'une terre que j'ai toujours cru mienne et que mon peuple laisse à la mondialisation des diversités' (5).

15 'Deux forces égales et opposées produisent un résultat nul. C'est ce qu'on vit au Québec. Une recette qui garantit immobilisme, confusion, pourrissement du climat social et échec final' (Paiement 2007: 4).

16 'De plus, aussi longtemps que je serai orphelin, j'aurai énormément de difficultés à bien intégrer les diversités présentes sur le territoire car j'ai peine à me définir moi-même, que je me sens menacé et que je n'ai pas tous les outils afin de vivre en pleine harmonie ... Je regrette mais je ne répondrai pas à vos attentes; pour le moment mes préoccupations se portent vers mon peuple et en ce qui concerne les diversités, c'est l'intégration à la culture québécoise et non l'inverse' (Émery 2007: 7–8).

17 'Aujourd'hui le peuple québécois a une identité. L'existence de cette commission en est un signe. Quand on se questionne comment recevoir les autres peuples, c'est parce qu'on est soi-même un peuple' (Charpentier 2007: 3).

18 'nous avons un problème identitaire résultant du fait que nous avons perdu une de nos bases. La religion n'est plus là' (Charpentier 2007: 2).

19 'Nation très accueillante et accommodante' (Denoncourt 2007: 3).

20 'l'égalité des sexes, la primauté de la langue française, la démocratie et la laïcité dans les sphères publiques de la société (3).

21 'Déjà notre société adulte démontre un affaiblissement avec sa perception de son identité et ses valeurs et semble être perdue dans un labyrinthe... Nous apercevrons dans quelques années une société au vrai sens du mot perdue où personne ne se reconnaît, une société qui aura une identité effacée au nom de la laïcité' (Nassr 2007: 3).

22 'En dehors de la métropole, le Québec est plus homogène, couve plus les traditions dites 'de souche', s'isole et se protège contre les ravages culturels de la mondialisation. Ce qu'il perd en manque de diversité, il gagne en intégrité. Le Québec a donc le meilleur des deux mondes parce qu'il possède en lui le moyen de reconnaître et de conserver son âme, tout en s'ouvrant sur un monde en évolution (Saywell 2007: 5).

23 'l'histoire de chacun de ces peuples' (El-Ghadban 2007: 5).

24 'La diversité n'a jamais fait disparaître les peuples' (El-Ghadban 2007: 14).

25 'Née à Québec, je suis comme on dit une Québécoise de souche. Mon ancêtre français, Louis Greffard, s'installa à l'Ile d'Orléans vers 1650. Il se maria avec une jeune fille née dans cette nouvelle colonie. Se succédèrent plusieurs générations jusqu'à mon père. Ce dernier, né à Sainte-Anne-de-Beaupré, a vécu toute sa vie à Québec. Son travail l'amena à arpenter tout le territoire québécois. Il a fait partie de cette race d'hommes qui furent coureurs des bois et bâtisseurs du pays' (Greffard 2007: 3).
26 'Nous, les êtres humains, ne sommes-nous pas un système complexe en perpétuel changement?' (Greffard 2007: 8).
27 'Comme on dit, il faut savoir ce que l'on veut: être réconforté dans ses certitudes ou être à l'aise avec les formes infinies de la réalité' (Greffard 2007: 11).
28 'Chacune d'elles m'ont révélé une facette de notre planète' (Greffard 2007: 14).
29 'Nous sommes tous liés et dans le même bateau. Nous faisons partie d'une immense chaîne ... ce qui arrive à l'un de nous affecte l'ensemble' (Greffard 2007: 15).
30 'Et bien si le Québec est si différent, il est encore un peu tôt pour le dire, il pourrait le prouver en devenant la première communauté planétaire à se débarrasser des concepts territoriaux, nationaux, culturels et religieux à partir desquels le monde s'est si mal construit depuis la nuit des temps. Acceptons le fait existentiel que nous sommes tous des nomades, des métis en quête de terre d'asile où l'on peut y trouver amour, travail, nourriture, repos et air pur. Regardons ce qui peut nous unir au-delà de la langue et du drapeau. Acceptons le fait que nous sommes toujours en mouvances et qu'il est dangereux de trop chercher à 'nous' définir une fois pour toutes. Comme si cela se pouvait. Les seuls points de départ et d'arrivée de nos existences sont notre naissance et notre descendance. Pour que cela continue d'être, construisons la première communauté d'intérêts planétaire du monde et surtout ne lui imposons pas de frontières' (Gignac 2007: 4).
31 Sunera Thobani's analysis of two such federal public consultations – the Immigration Policy Review and the Social Security Review in 1994 – concludes that the process only reinforced the 'exaltation' of the dominant group, further marginalizing Canada's racialized others and representing Aboriginal peoples and immigrants 'as outside the nation' (Thobani 2007: 212).

5: The B-T Report 'Open Secularism' Model and the Supreme Court of Canada Decisions on Freedom of Religion and Religious Accommodation

1 Regarding the relationship between the four principles of secularism, the Commission has the following to say: 'How can we conceive of a relationship

between the two purposes and the two structures in a system of secularism? We can essentially envision it as a relationship between aims and means, while recognizing that the means here are indispensible, or we can consider these four facets, both neutrality and separation and the two purposes, as values in themselves. This is a philosophical difference that we do not have to settle here. The fact remains that considered in either manner, the four principles can come into conflict and engender dilemmas that must be resolved' (Bouchard and Taylor 2008: 137).

2 Among the briefs promoting a concept of secularism based on the French model, see, for example, the one that was presented to the Bouchard-Taylor Commission by the Mouvement laïque québécois, *Pour une gestion laïque de la diversité culturelle*, September 2007 (available on the Commission's website at http://www.accommodements.qc.ca/documentation/memoires.html). One can also consult the positions of the MLQ at: www.mlq.qc.ca/.

3 On the concept of secularism (laïcité) in France, see Messner, Prélot, and Woehrling (2003: 421), as well as Woehrling (1998: 101). In fact, the French courts have traditionally adopted the same position as the Canadian courts regarding the wearing of religious signs in public schools, taking the position that this is not incompatible with the principle of secularism, and, to the contrary, should be authorized in the name of religious freedom, unless particular circumstances justify prohibiting it. The new French statute that prohibits the 'conspicuous' display of religious signs in public schools (Loi n° 2004-228 du 15 mars 2004, art. 1 *Journal officiel* du 17 mars 2004 en vigueur le 1er septembre 2004) was legally justified, not by the principle of secularism, but by the existence of circumstances endangering public security: the pressure exerted on young girls coming from immigrant families to wear the veil, communitarian grouping along ethnic lines in the recreation areas and school cafeterias, the tensions, conflicts, and divisions engendered by demands related to ethnicity and religion in the schools, etc. According to the French government, given these circumstances the wearing of the veil in public schools constitutes a practice that threatens and disturbs public order. To justify the prohibition of the Islamic veil in public schools in Quebec, there would have to be comparable circumstances, which does not seem to be the case.

4 In France, the first paragraph of Article 2 of the Constitution of 4 October 1958 proclaims: 'France shall be an indivisible, secular, democratic and social Republic. It shall ensure the equality of all citizens before the law, without any distinction of origin, race or religion. It shall respect all beliefs.'

5 The international instruments for the protection of human rights that protect freedom of religion are opposed to a concept of secularism that would claim to exclude religion from the public sphere and to restrict it to a purely private and intimate space. Thus, Article 18 of the International Covenant on Civil and Political Rights sets out as follows the components of freedom of religion: '1. Everyone shall have the right to freedom of thought, conscience and religion. This right shall include freedom to have or to adopt a religion or belief of his choice, and freedom, either individually or in community with others *and in public or private*, to manifest his religion or belief in worship, observance, practice and teaching' (emphasis mine). The United Nations Human Rights Committee has put forward several general observations which contain the guiding principles for the significance and interpretation to be given to specific articles in the Covenant. In *General Comment No. 22 on Freedom of Thought, Conscience and Religion*, the Committee has notably drawn attention to the following points: '[...] The freedom to manifest religion or belief in worship, observance, practice and teaching encompasses a broad range of acts. The concept of worship extends to ritual and ceremonial acts giving direct expression to belief, as well as various practices integral to such acts, including the building of places of worship, the use of ritual formulae and objects, the display of symbols, and the observance of holidays and days of rest. The observance and practice of religion or belief may include not only ceremonial acts but also such customs as the observance of dietary regulations, the wearing of distinctive clothing or headcoverings, participation in rituals associated with certain stages of life, and the use of a particular language customarily spoken by a group. In addition, the practice and teaching of religion or belief includes acts integral to the conduct by religious groups of their basic affairs, such as the freedom to choose their religious leaders, priests and teachers, the freedom to establish seminaries or religious schools and the freedom to prepare and distribute religious texts or publications' (par. 4).

6 The third and fourth recommendations contained in the brief of the Mouvement laïque québécois read as follows : 'In applying secular principles, no exemptions to the democratically adopted public norms should be granted for reasons of religious beliefs or metaphysical convictions ... The Canadian Charter of Rights and Freedoms should be amended to respond to the new needs of our society, to better ensure its secular nature and to correct misguided court decisions regarding religious accommodations; Québec should take the initiative to propose this amendment.'

7 The Commission's report gives the following definition of 'open' secularism: '[Open secularism] recognizes the need for the State to be neutral

(statutes and public institutions must not favour any religion or secular conception) but it also acknowledges the importance for some people of the spiritual dimension of existence and, consequently, the protection of freedom of conscience and religion.' (Bouchard Taylor 2008: 140). The Commission recognizes that while there is fairly broad agreement among the public organizations and groups from civil society that expressed an opinion on this model of open secularism, this does not, however, indicate a true consensus within Québec society on this question. Quite the reverse, the Commission's public hearings revealed that there is profound disagreement on the policy directions that Québec should now adopt in respect of secularism. Nevertheless, the Commission affirms that it is the model of open secularism that should continue to be applied because it best allows us to respect both the equality of persons and their freedom of conscience and religion and thus to achieve the two fundamental purposes of secularism. (Bouchard and Taylor 2008: 141).

8 *Constitution Act, 1867*, 30 & 31 Vict., R.-U., c. 3; L.R.C. (1985), App. II, n° 5.
9 Jean-Pierre Proulx et José Woehrling, 'La restructuration du système scolaire québécois et la modification de l'article 93 de la *Loi constitutionnelle de 1867* (1997), 31 *Revue juridique Thémis*, 399–510.
10 French courts consider that the principle of secularism does not tolerate the right of public employees, teachers as well as non-teaching staff in the domain of public education, to express their religious beliefs while carrying out their functions; notably, 'by wearing a sign meant to manifest [their] adherence to a religion': Conseil d'État, 3 May 2000, *Mlle Marteaux*, Journal officiel du 23 juin 2000, p. 9471. For an examination of the French situation, see Gonzales (2006).
11 The European Court of Human Rights seems to consider that the limitation of religious freedom of teachers in public schools is only justified to the extent that the principle of neutrality or the religious freedom of students or their parents are being compromised, taking into account the particular context of the case in question, in particular the age of the students and the more or less ostentatious nature of the religious sign in question; see, in particular, *Dahlab* v. *Switzerland*, no 42393/98, 15 February 2001, European Court of Human Rights (2nd section). For an analysis of this decision, see Gonzalez (2006), 166ff.
12 *Grant* v. *Canada (Attorney General)*, [1995] 1 F.C. 158 (Federal Court – trial division); the decision was confirmed in appeal: (1995) 125 D.L.R. (4th) 556 (F.C.A.).
13 About the situation in the United States, see Schachter (1993); Burkholder (1989); Bastian (1991). The same situation exists in Germany. In a 2003

decision, the Constitutional Court ruled that the Länder enjoy a wide margin of appreciation when defining the balance between religious freedom of teachers and the principle of religious neutrality of public authorities, in particular in the school system, going so far as to allow them, if they so decide, to prohibit the wearing of all religious signs by teachers during the exercise of their functions. Currently, this question is regulated in varying ways by the German Länder, some prohibiting religious signs in a general way, others providing for a contextual examination of each specific case, with prohibition only in cases where it is clearly demonstrated that such an attitude would have negative effects on the religious freedom of students or their parents or on the religious neutrality of the school. About the situation in Germany, see Langenfeld and Rome (2005).
14 Regarding the possibility in a federation, and particularly in Canada, of the interpretation of human rights and freedoms varying from one province to another, see Woehrling (2000). It has happened that the Canadian Supreme Court deemed as justified certain limitations to the freedom of expression resulting from the *Charter of the French language* L.Q. 1977, c. 5; L.R.Q., c. C-1, while indicating that it would probably not have perceived them as such if they had resulted from the laws of a different Canadian province; see: *Ford* v. *A.G. for Québec*, [1988] 2 S.C.R. 712. In this case, the Court accepted that freedom of commercial expression can be limited by imposing the predominant use of French in commercial signs, taking into account the vulnerability of the French language.
15 See note 4 above.
16 'Congress shall make no law respecting an establishment of religion, or prohibiting the free exercise thereof.' United States of America, Constitution (1787), Amendment 1 (1791).
17 Indeed, the Supreme Court considers that *freedom of religion* implicitly includes a requirement of *equality* in matters of religion. It clearly adopted this point of view in its first two decisions regarding freedom of religion, the *R.* v. *Big M Drug Mart Ltd.*, [1985] 1 S.C.R. 295 and *R.* v. *Edwards Books*, [1986] 2 S.C.R. 713 decisions, both rendered at a time when Section 15 of the Canadian Charter, guaranteeing the right to equality, was not yet in force. In the case of *Big M Drug Mart*, on pp. 336 and 337, Judge Dickson considered that an infringement of freedom of religion can result from either a state coercion that obliges someone to, or prevents someone from, conforming to religious dictates, or inequality in the treatment of one religion as compared to another.
18 In the *Big M Drug Mart* case, the objective of the contested federal law, which prohibited the opening of retail businesses on Sundays, was to force the entire population to carry out a Christian religious observance, and

this was incompatible with the religious freedom guaranteed by the Canadian Charter; the law was therefore invalidated. In the *Edwards Books* case, the objective of the Ontario statute, which prohibited stores from opening on Sunday in much the same manner, was to procure a weekly common day of rest for retail employees. Obviously the Court considered this to be a legitimate legislative objective. It validated the law as restricting religious freedom in a reasonable and justifiable way. Furthermore, if it was to be concluded that there was no duty of neutrality resulting from Section 2a of the Canadian Charter, such a duty would result from Section 15 that prohibits discriminatory distinctions based on religion. In the same vein, aside from Sections 2a and 15 of the Charter, the duty of neutrality of the state concerning religion also follows from Section 27 on multiculturalism. Indeed, to the extent that religion is part of culture, the respect of multiculturalism is incompatible with the act of favouring certain religions over others. This is what Judge Dickson concluded in the *Big M Drug Mart* case, on pp. 337–8.

19 *Zylberberg v. Sudbury Board of Education* (1988) 65 O.R. (2d) 641 (Ont. C.A.) leave to appeal to the Supreme Court dismissed.

20 *Canadian Civil Liberties Association v. Ontario (Minister of Education)* (1990) 71 O.R. (2d) 341; 65 D.L.R. (4th) 1 (Ont. C.A.), leave to appeal to the Supreme Court dismissed.

21 It should be pointed out that the Ontario Court interpreted freedom of religion in a way that is more restrictive than required by international standards. Indeed, it seems that the existence of a possibility of exemption regarding religious instruction, or having the option of either religious instruction or a neutral and objective cultural and moral instruction, are generally seen as measures that ensure conformity with religious freedom as guaranteed in international instruments; see the *General Comment No. 22 (48) (Sec. 18) on Freedom of Thought, Conscience and Religion* of the United Nations Committee on Human Rights, Doc. N.U. CCPR./C/21/Rev. 1/add.4, 20 July 1993, par.6.

22 The principles asserted in these two decisions are obviously not applicable to private schools. To the contrary, in the case of *R. v. Jones*, [1986] 2 S.C.R. 284, the Supreme Court interpreted Section 2a of the Canadian Charter as guaranteeing the right of parents to not send their children to public school and to give them a religious education in a private school or at home, as long as such an education was 'appropriate.'

23 *Adler v. Ontario*, [1996] 3 S.C.R. 609, p. 705 (Judge Sopinka).

24 *Congrégation des témoins de Jéhovah de St-Jérôme-Lafontaine v. Lafontaine (Village)*, [2004] 2 S.C.R. 650.

138   Notes to pages 94–6

25 Ibid. Par. 65 (Judge LeBel).
26 The same reasoning was used by the Ontario Court of Appeal to conclude that the recitation of The Lord's Prayer at the beginning of municipal council sessions, an initiative of the mayor, who was acting as presiding officer, entailed a coercion incompatible with religious freedom on the members of the council and the people attending the session who had to leave the room or stay seated during the prayer to indicate that they were not participating in it. The Court did not take into account the fact that the people in question here were adults, less impressionable and less psychologically vulnerable than school-age children. See *Freitag* v. *Penetanguishene* [1999] 179 D.L.R. (4th) 150 (Ont. C.A.).
27 The phrase of the preamble of the Canadian Charter: 'Whereas Canada is founded upon principles that recognize the supremacy of God ...' has not played a role of any significance until now in the case-law, in the defining of the nature of the relationship between the state and religions or the content of religious freedom. One has to remember that the Preamble of an Act or a Constitution can only be used in an interpretive manner and only to interpret a possible ambiguity in the text.
28 A number of authors have expressed the opinion that the principle of neutrality recognized in Canada should be viewed as less rigorous than the principle of non-establishment in the United States; see, among many, Hogg (2005: 945); Ryder (2005: 169); and Horwitz (1996: 60–1): '... aid to religion should be constrained by only two considerations. It must not create an "element of religious compulsion" on the part of any believers or non-believers in a given faith. Also, while government aid may properly create the impression that the state is supportive of religion as it is of other mediating institutions, it should not create the impression that it has singled out a particular faith, or religiosity over non-religiosity, for endorsement. Endorsement, even if it does not compel behaviour on the part of the minority, defeats the pluralism and multiculturalism that are a central part of religion's value to society' (footnotes omitted).
29 In *Big M Drug Mart* (cited in note 17 above), on pp. 340–1, Judge Dickson expressly leaves open the question of whether the Canadian Charter *permits* the state to financially support private religious institutions; neither was the question clearly decided in *Adler* v. *Ontario*, (cited in note 23 above), in which the Supreme Court nevertheless ruled that the Canadian Charter did not *oblige* the state to provide a support of this kind. In practice, several Canadian provinces, notably Québec, finance private religious schools to a degree that varies with each province.
30 In other words, when a law that is applied in a neutral and uniform manner has a prejudicial effect on the religious freedom of certain individuals,

it can no longer be considered neutral, and accommodation is therefore required, precisely to re-establish the neutrality of the law concerned (except if such accommodation entails an excessive constraint on the public interest or on someone else's rights). It is therefore the principle of state religious neutrality itself that, in certain cases, calls for reasonable accommodations.

31 *R. v. Videoflicks Ltd.*, (1985) 14 D.L.R. (4th) 10 (Ont. C.A.).
32 In its report, the Commission recommends the removal of the crucifix hanging above the president's chair in the Québec National Assembly because it suggests that a 'special closeness' exists between legislative power and the religion of the majority (Bouchard and Taylor 2008: 152–3).

6: Conclusion: Religion, Culture, and the State

1 Léger Marketing survey conducted by online questionnaire May 13–16 of 1,003 Québecers accurate within 3.9 percentage points, 19 times out of 20.
2 See Marian Scott (2009), 'More Québecers see immigrants as threat: poll,' *Montreal Gazette* (23 May 2009).
3 David Hume called that interpersonal bonding 'sentiment,' while Adam Smith dubbed it 'sympathy.' Sympathy is, for Smith, just the harmony of sentiments to create a common feeling. Cf. Smith (1759; 1790), vol. 1, pt.1, sec.1, chap.1, p. 6.
4 Humans are basically social creatures, not autonomous, self-regarding possessive individualists. They are deeply interconnected by networks and organized by their attachments into the knitted fabric of society reinforced by their social institutions (Etzioni 1998; Aronson 2003).
5 Immigration and Refugee Board of Canada (20 September 2007), 'Somalia: Prevalence of forced or arranged marriages in Somalia; consequences for a young woman who refuses to participate in a forced or arranged marriage,' SOM10Z612.E. UNHCR: RefWorld. http://www.unhcr.org/refworld/docid/47ce6d7a2b.html. See also Musse (2004).
6 Travel report published by Foreign Affairs and International Trade Canada, 22 August 2007.
7 A Symposium on non-consensual marriage, 'The Right to Choose', was held in Toronto in June 2008. http://www.awid.org/Issues-and-Analysis/Library/Selected-proceedings-from-The-Right-to-Choose-international-symposium-on-non-consensual-marriage-Toronto-Canada-June

References

Adams, Michael, with Amy Langstaff (2007). *Unlikely Utopia: The Surprising Triumph of Canadian Pluralism.* Toronto: Viking Canada.
Allen, Anita L. (2008). 'Undressing Difference: The *Hijāb* in the West.' Philadelphia: University of Pennsylvania Law School. NELLCO, http://lsr.nellco.org/upenn wps/220.
Althusser, Louis (1971). 'Ideology and Ideological State Apparatuses: Notes Towards an Investigation.' In *Lenin and Philosophy and Other Essays*, 123–73. Trans. Ben Brewster. New York: Monthly Review Press.
Anctil, Pierre (1988). *Le rendez-vous manqué: Les Juifs de Montréal face au Québec de l'entre-deux-guerres.* Québec: Institut québécois de recherche sur la culture.
Anctil, Pierre (1996). 'La trajectoire interculturelle du Québec: La société distincte vue à travers le prisme de l'immigration.' In *Langues, cultures et valeurs au Canada à l'aube du XXIe siècle (Language, Culture and Values in Canada at the Dawn of the 21st Century)*, 133–54. Ed. André Lapierre, Patricia Smart, et Pierre Savard. Ottawa: International Council for Canadian Studies and Carleton University Press.
Anctil, Pierre (2005). 'Défi et gestion de l'immigration internationale au Québec.' Special issue: 'Le Québec, une autre identité: Dynamisme d'une identité.' *Cités* 23: 43–55.
Anctil, Pierre (2007). 'Quel accommodement raisonnable?' *Éthique publique* 9(1): 186–91.
Anctil, Pierre, Ira Robinson, and Gérard Bouchard (2000). *Juifs et Canadiens français dans la société québécoise.* Sillery, Québec: Septentrion.
Anderson, Benedict (1991). *Imagined Communities: Reflections on the Origin and Spread of Nationalism.* London: Verso.
Aronson, E. (2003). *The Social Animal.* 9th ed. New York: Worth Publishers.

Atwood, Margaret (1972). *Survival: A Thematic Guide to Canadian Literature*. Toronto: House of Anansi Press.

Barnett, Michael, and Raymond Duvall (2005). 'Power in International Politics.' *International Organization* 59 (winter): 43.

Bastian, Holly M. (1991). 'Case Comment: Religious Garb Statutes and Title VII: An Uneasy Coexistence.' *Georgetown Law Journal* 80: 211.

Baubérot, Jean (2000). *Histoire de la laïcité française*. Paris: Presses universitaires de France.

Baubérot, Jean (2004). *Laïcité 1905–2005: Entre passion et raison*. Paris: Seuil.

Beaud, Stéphane, and Michel Pialoux (2003). 'Violences sociale: Genèse des nouvelles classes dangereuses.' In *Violences urbaines, violences sociales: Genèse des nouvelles classes sociales dangereuses*, 357–64. Paris: Fayard.

Beiner, Ronald (2003). *Liberalism, Nationalism, Citizenship: Essays on the Problem of Political Community*. Vancouver: University of British Columbia Press.

Bellil, Samira (2002). *Dans l'enfer des tournantes* (In gang-rape hell). Paris: Gallimard.

Benhabib, Seyla (2004). *The Rights of Others: Aliens, Residents, and Citizens*. Cambridge and New York: Cambridge University Press.

Bernard-Patel, Sylvie (2008). 'A Comparative Study on Islam and Identity in Britain and France.' Presented at the international conference, Representing Islam: Comparative Perspectives. University of Manchester, 5–6 September.

Bisson, Marcien (2007). 'Mémoire.' Brief submitted to the Consultation Commission on Accommodation Practices Related to Cultural Differences. http://www.accommodements.qc.ca/documentation/memoires/Jonquiere/bisson-marcien.pdf.

Bissoondath, Neil (1994). *Selling Illusions: The Cult of Multiculturalism in Canada*. Toronto: Penguin Books.

Blattberg, Charles (2003). *Shall We Dance? A Patriotic Politics for Canada*. Montréal: McGill-Queen's University Press.

Bosset, Pierre (1995). *Le pluralisme religieux au Québec: Un défi d'éthique sociale. Document soumis à la réflexion publique*. Montréal: Commission des droits de la personne et des droits de la jeunesse.

Bosset, Pierre (2005). *Réflexion sur la portée et les limites de l'obligation d'accommodement raisonnable en matière religieuse*. Montréal: Commission des droits de la personne et des droits de la jeunesse.

Bouchard, Gérard (2001). *Genèse des nations et cultures du Nouveau Monde: Essai d'histoire comparée*. Montréal: Boréal.

Bouchard, Gérard, et Alain Roy (2007). *La culture québécoise est-elle en crise?* Montréal: Boréal.

Bouchard, Gérard, et Charles Taylor (2007a). *Accommodements et différences: Vers un terrain d'entente: La parole aux citoyens*. Document de consultation. Montréal: Commission de consultation sur les pratiques d'accommodements reliées aux différences culturelles.

Bouchard, Gérard, and Charles Taylor (2007b). *Accommodation and Differences: Seeking Common Ground: Québecers Speak Out*. Consultation Document. Québec : Gouvernement du Québec. http://www.accommodements.qc.ca/documentation/document-consultation-en.pdf.

Bouchard, Gérard, and Charles Taylor (2008). *Fonder l'avenir: Le temps de la conciliation. Rapport de la Commission de consultation sur les pratiques d'accommodement reliées aux différences culturelles*. Montréal: Commission de consultation sur les pratiques d'accommodements reliées aux différences culturelles; 'Building the Future: A Time for Reconciliation.' Québec: Gouvernement de Québec. http://www.accommodements.qc.ca/documentation/rapports/rapport-final-abrege-en.pdf.

Boulangé, Antoine (2004). 'The Hijäb, Racism and the State.' *International Socialism Journal*, 102. http://pubs.socialistreviewindex.org.uk/isj102/boulange.htm.

Bowen, R. (2003). *Why the French Don't Like Headscarves: Islam, the State, and Public Space*. Princeton, NJ: Princeton University Press.

Burkholder, John David (1989). 'Religious Rights of Teachers in Public Education.' *Journal of Law and Education* 18.

Burnet, Jean R., and Howard Palmer (1988). *Coming Canadians: An Introduction to a History of Canada's Peoples*. Toronto: McClelland and Stewart.

Carens, Joseph H. (2005). *Démocratie, multiculturalisme et hijäb*. ESPRIT 311 (2 January): 54-61.

Charland, Maurice (1987). 'Constitutive Rhetoric: The Case of the Peuple Québécois.' *Quarterly Journal of Speech* 73 (2): 133– 50.

Charpentier, Serge (2007). 'De la différence et de la non-différence et de l'identité et de la non-identité.' Brief submitted to the Consultation Commission on Accommodation Practices Related to Cultural Differences. http://www.accommodements.qc.ca/documentation/memoires/Montreal-d/charpentier-serge06-0359-d-00.pdf.

Cohen, Andrew (2007). *The Unfinished Canadian: The People We Are*. Toronto: McClelland and Stewart.

Cohen, Anthony P. (2000). 'Peripheral Vision: Nationalism, National Identity and the Objective Correlative in Scotland.' In *Signifying Identities: Anthropological Perspectives on Boundaries and Contested Values*, 145–69. Ed. Anthony Cohen and P. Cohen. London: Routledge.

Day, Richard J.F. (2000). *Multiculturalism and the History of Canadian Diversity.* Toronto: University of Toronto Press.

Delisle, Esther (1993). *The Traitor and the Jew: Anti-Semitism and Extremist Right-wing Nationalism in Québec from 1929 to 1939.* Montreal: Davies.

Deltombe, Thomas (2005). *L'Islam imaginaire: La construction méditique de l'islamophobie en France, 1975–2005.* Paris: La Découverte.

Denoncourt, Gisèle (2007). 'S'accommoder, certainement. Mais holà, préservons nos valeurs communes!' Brief submitted to the Consultation Commission on Accommodation Practices Related to Cultural Differences. http://www.accommodements.qc.ca/documentation/memoires/Drummond ville/denoncourt-gisele-s-accommoder-certainement-mais-hola-preservons-nos-valeurs-communes.pdf.

Djavann, Chahdortt (2003). *Bas les voiles!* Paris: Gallimard.

Dowd, Marc-André (2006). 'L'accommodement raisonnable: Éviter les dérapages.' *Le Devoir*, 21 November.

Dupret, Baudouin (2007). 'Legal Pluralism, Plurality of Laws, and Legal Practices: Theories, Critiques, and Praxiological Re-specification.' *European Journal of Legal Studies.* www.ejls.eu/1/14UK.pdf.

Eisenstadt, Shmuel N. (2007). 'Modes of Religious Pluralism under Conditions of Globalization.' In *Democracy and Human Rights in Multicultural Societies.* Ed. Matthias Koenig and Paul de Guchteneire. Aldershot, UK: Ashgate/UNESCO.

El-Ghadban, Yara (2007). 'Vivre le "je me souviens" au pluriel.' Brief submitted to the Consultation Commission on Accommodation Practices Related to Cultural Differences. http://www.accommodements.qc.ca/documentation/memoires/Montreal/el-ghadban-yara-vivre-le-je-me-souviens-au-pluriel-Montreal.pdf.

El Guindi, Fadwa (1999). *Veil: Modesty, Privacy and Resistance.* Oxford and New York: Berg.

Émery, Michel (2007). 'Mémoire.' Brief submitted to the Consultation Commission on Accommodation Practices Related to Cultural Differences. http://www.accommodements.qc.ca/documentation/memoires/Montreal-d/Emery-michel06-0085-pe-00.pdf.

Etzioni, A. (1998). *The Essential Communitarian Reader.* Lanham, MD: Rowan and Littlefield.

Faulks, Keith (2000). *Citizenship.* New York: Routledge.

Fournier, Marcel (2001). 'Québec Sociology and Québec Society: The Construction of a Collective Identity.' *Canadian Journal of Sociology* 26: 3.

Fournier, Marcel (2002). 'Québec Sociology: A Discipline and Its Object.' *The American Sociologist* 33 (1): 42–54.
Franken, Robert E. (1998). *Human Motivation*. 4th ed. Pacific Grove, CA: Brooks/Cole Publishing.
Freiwald, Bina Toledo (2002). 'Nation and Self-Narration: A View from Québec/Quebec.' *Canadian Literature* 172: 17–38.
Gignac, Benoît (2007). 'Mémoire "idéaliste."' Brief submitted to the Consultation Commission on Accommodation Practices Related to Cultural Differences. http://www.accommodements.qc.ca/documentation/memoires/St-Jerome/gignac-benoit-memoire-presente-a-la-ccpardc.pdf.
Godfrey, Hannah (2003). 'Schools' bid for headscarf ban widens French divide.' *The Observer*, 15 June.
Godin, André (2007). 'Des grands enjeux éthiques pour mieux encadrer les accommodements raisonnables. Présentation aux commissaires d'un mémoire sur les accommodements raisonnables.' Brief submitted to the Consultation Commission on Accommodation Practices Related to Cultural Differences. http://www.accommodements.qc.ca/documentation/memoires/Sherbrooke/godin-andre-des-grands-enjeux-ethiques-pour-mieux-encadrer-les-accommodements-raisonnables.pdf.
Gonzalez, Gérard (2006). 'L'exigence de neutralité des services publics.' In *Laïcité, liberté de religion et Convention européenne des droits de l'homme* (Actes du colloque organisé le 18 novembre 2005 par l'Institut de droit européen des droits de l'homme), 153–69. Ed. Gérard Gonzalez. Bruxelles: Bruylant.
Gopnik, Adam (2009a). *Angels and Ages: A Short Book about Darwin, Lincoln, and Modern Life*. New York: Knopf.
Gopnik, Adam (2009b). 'The Return of the Native: A Public Intellectual Remakes Himself as a Public Servant.' *The New Yorker*, 7 September.
Gouvernement du Québec (1990). *Au Québec pour bâtir ensemble, Énoncé de politique en matière d'immigration et d'intégration*. Ministère des Communautés culturelles et de l'Immigration du Québec. Québec: Gouvernement du Québec.
Gouvernement du Québec (1991). *Accord Canada-Québec relatif à l'intégration et à l'admission des aubains*. Ministère des Communautés culturelles et de l'Immigration du Québec. Québec: Gouvernement du Québec.
Greffard, Hélène (2006). 'Voyage d'une Québécoise de souche en terrain étranger.' Brief submitted to the Consultation Commission on Accommodation Practices Related to Cultural Differences. http://www.accommodements.qc.ca/documentation/memoires/Montreal/greffard-helene-voyage-d-une-Québecoise-de-souche-en-terrain-etranger.pdf.

Gresh, Alain (2004a). *L'islam, la République et le monde.* Paris: Fayard.
Gresh, Alain (2004b). 'A Concept of Origins.' *Le Monde diplomatique,* 23 September.
Gros-Louis, Max (2007). 'One-Onti: an'onwentsa: la rencontre.' Brief submitted to the Consultation Commission on Accommodation Practices Related to Cultural Differences. http://www.accommodements.qc.ca/documentation/memoires/Québec/gros-louis-max-one-onti-an-onwentsa-la-rencontre.pdf.
Habermas, Jürgen (1991). *The Structural Transformation of the Public Sphere: An Inquiry into a Category of Bourgeois Society.* Cambridge, MA: MIT Press.
Handler, Richard (1988). *Nationalism and the Politics of Culture in Québec.* Madison: University of Wisconsin Press.
Hegel, G.W.F. (1977). *Phenomenology of Spirit.* Trans. A.V. Miller. Oxford: Oxford University Press.
Heinrich, Jeff, and Valérie Dufour (2008). *Circus Québécus: Sous le chapiteau de la Commission Bouchard-Taylor.* Montreal: Éditions du Boréal.
Hogg, Peter W. (2005). *Constitutional Law of Canada.* Scarborough, ON: Thomson-Carswell.
Horwitz, Paul (1996). 'The Sources and Limits of Freedom of Religion in a Liberal Democracy: Section 2(a) and Beyond.' *University of Toronto Faculty of Law Review* 54 (1): 60–1.
Hurd, Elizabeth Shakman (2008). *The Politics of Secularism in International Relations.* Princeton, NJ: Princeton University Press.
Ignatieff, Michael (1993). *Blood and Belonging: Journeys into the New Nationalism.* New York: Farrar, Straus and Giroux.
Joppke, Christian (2009). *Veil: Mirror of Identity.* London: Polity Press.
Keaton, Trica Danielle (2006). *Muslim Girls and the Other France: Race, Identity Politics, and Social Exclusion.* Bloomington and Indianapolis: Indiana University Press.
Kelley, Ninette, and Michael J. Trebilcock (1998). *The Making of the Mosaic: A History of Canadian Immigration Policy.* Toronto: University of Toronto Press.
Kertzer, Jonathan (1998). *Worrying the Nation: Imagining a National Literature in English Canada.* Toronto: University of Toronto Press.
Knowles, Valerie (2007). *Strangers at Our Gates: Canadian Immigration and Immigration Policy, 1540–2007.* Toronto: Dundurn Press.
Kymlicka, William (1995a). *Multicultural Citizenship: A Liberal Theory of Minority Rights.* Oxford: Clarendon Press.
Kymlicka, William, ed. (1995b). *The Rights of Minority Cultures.* Oxford: Oxford University Press.
Kymlicka, William (1998). *Finding Our Way: Rethinking Ethnocultural Relations in Canada.* Toronto: Oxford University Press.

Kymlicka, William (2001). 'From Enlightenment Cosmopolitanism to Liberal Nationalism.' In *Politics in the Vernacular: Nationalism, Multiculturalism and Citizenship*. Ed. William Kymlicka. New York: Oxford University Press.

Laborde, Cécile (2006). 'Female Autonomy, Education and the *Hijäb*.' *Critical Review of International Social and Political Philosophy* 9 (3): 351–77.

Laborde, Cécile (2008). *Critical Republicanism: The Hijäb Controversy and Political Philosophy*. Oxford: Oxford University Press.

Langenfeld, Christine, and Sarah Mohsen (2005). 'Developments– Germany: The Teacher Headscarf Case.' *International Journal of Constitutional Law* 3 (86).

Langlais, Jacques, and David Rome (1991). *Jews and French Québecers: Two Hundred Years of Shared History*. Waterloo, ON: Wilfred Laurier University Press.

Lapidus, Steven (2004). 'The Forgotten Hasidim: Rabbis and Rebbes in Prewar Canada.' *Canadian Jewish Studies* 12: 1–30.

Leoussi, Athena S., and Steven Grosby. eds. (2007). *Nationalism and Ethnosymbolism: History, Culture and Ethnicity in the Formation of Nations*. New York: Columbia University Press; Edinburgh: Edinburgh University Press.

Levy, Bernard-Henry (2004). 'Off with Their Headscarves.' *The Guardian*, 1 February.

Lewis, Bernard (2003). '"I'm Right, You're Wrong, Go to Hell": Religions and the Meeting of Civilization.' *Atlantic Monthly*, May.

Lisée, Jean-Francois (2007). 'Pour un nouvel équilibre entre tous les "nous" Québécois.' Brief submitted to the Consultation Commission on Accommodation Practices Related to Cultural Differences. http://www.accommodements.qc.ca/documentation/memoires/A-N-Montreal/lisee-jean-francois.pdf.

Lorcerie, Françoise (2001). 'L'étranger face au droit et au regard du droit.' In *L'étranger et le droit de la famille : Pluralité ethnique, pluralisme juridique*. Ed. Philippe Kahn. Paris: La Documentation française.

Maclure, Jocelyn (2003). *Québec Identity: The Challenge of Pluralism*. Trans. Peter Feldstein. Montréal and Kingston: McGill-Queen's University Press.

Mahmood, Saba (2005). *The Politics of Piety: The Islamic Revival and the Feminist Subject*. Princeton, NJ: Princeton University Press.

Maruani, N. (2009). 'The Hijäb, a Political Weapon and Form of Sexual Abuse, Should Be Outlawed.' Washington, DC: Middle East Media Research Institute. www.memri.org/french.

May, Stephen, and Mehta Deepa (2007). 'Forced Marriages/Non-Consensual Marriages.' Report to the OCASI Professional Development Conference. Toronto, October.

May, Stephen, Tariq Modood, and Judith Squires, eds. (2004). *Ethnicity, Nationality and Minority Rights*. Cambridge: Cambridge University Press.

McGoldrick, Dominic (2006). *Human Rights and Religion –The Islamic Headscarf Debate in Europe.* Oxford and Portland, OR: Hart Publishing.

Mead, George Herbert (1936). *Movements of Thought in the Nineteenth Century.* Ed. Merritt H. Moore. Chicago: Chicago University Press.

Meadwell, Hudson (1993). 'Transitions to Independence and Ethnic Nationalist Mobilization.' In *Politics and Rationality*, 191–213. Ed. William James Booth, Patrick James, and Hudson Meadwell. Cambridge: Cambridge University Press.

Messner, Francis , Pierre-Henri Prélot, and Jean-Marie Woehrling (2003). *Traité de droit français des religions.* Paris: Litec.

Modood, Tariq (2000). 'The Place of Muslims in British Secular Multiculturalism.' In *Modern Europe, or Euro-Islam: Politics, Culture, and Citizenship in the Age of Globalization*, 113–30. Ed. N. AlSayyad and M. Castells (2002). Lanham, MD: Lexington Books.

Modood, Tariq (2005). *Multicultural Politics: Racism, Ethnicity and Muslims in Britain.* Edinburgh: Edinburgh University Press.

Modood, Tariq (2008). 'The multicultural state we're in: Muslims, "multiculture" and the "civic re-balancing" of British multiculturalism.' Presented at the international conference, Representing Islam: Comparative Perspectives. University of Manchester, 5–6 September.

Modood, Tariq, A. Triandafyllidou, and Z. Zapata-Barreroet, eds. (2006). *Multiculturalism, Muslims and Citizenship: A European Approach.* London: Routledge.

Montaigne, Michel de (1991). *The Complete Essays.* Trans. M.A. Screech. New York: Penguin.

Musse Ahmed, Sadia (2004). 'Traditions of Marriage and the Household.' In *Somalia– The Untold Story: The War Through the Eyes of Somali Women.* Ed. Judith Gardner and Judy El Bushra. London: Pluto Press.

Nassr, Fadia (2007). 'Une province unique de son genre.' Brief submitted to the Consultation Commission on Accommodation Practices Related to Cultural Differences. http://www.accommodements.qc.ca/documentation/memoires/Laval-d/nassr-fadia13-0021-de-00.pdf.

Norton, Anne (2004). *95 Theses on Politics, Culture and Method.* New Haven: Yale University Press.

Parekh, B. (2000). *Rethinking Multiculturalism: Cultural Diversity and Political Theory.* Houndmills, UK and London: Macmillan Press.

Paiement, Alain C (2007). 'Mémoire.' Brief submitted to the Consultation Commission on Accommodation Practices Related to Cultural Differences. http://www.accommodements.qc.ca/documentation/memoires/Gatineau-d/paiement-alain07-0006-de-00.pdf.

Parenteau, François (2002). *Qui est nous?* Québec: Les Productions Virage.
Park, Bernadette, and Charles M. Judd (2005). 'Rethinking the Link between Categorization and Prejudice within the Social Cognition Perspective.' *Personality and Social Psychology Review* 9(2): 108–30.
Pena-Ruiz, Henri (2005). *Histoire de la laïcité: Genèse d'un idéal.* Paris: Gallimard.
Probyn, Elspeth (1996). *Outside Belongings.* New York: Routledge.
Proulx, Jean-Pierre, et José Woehrling (1997). 'La restructuration du système scolaire québécois et la modification de l'article 93 de la Loi constitutionnelle de 1867.' *Revue juridique Thémis* 31: 399–510.
Rachad, Antonius (2008). 'Representing Muslims and Arabs in Canadian Newspapers.' Presented at the international conference, Representing Islam: Comparative Perspectives. University of Manchester. 5–6 September.
Rawls, John (1997). 'The Idea of Public Reason Revisited.' In *John Rawls: Collected Papers,* 573–615. Ed. Samuel Freeman. Cambridge, MA: Harvard University Press.
Renaud, Jean (2001). *Ils sont maintenant d'ici! Les dix premières années au Québec des immigrants admis en 1989.* Québec: Publications du Québec.
Renaut, Alain, and Alain Touraine (2005). *Un debat sur la laïcité.* Paris: Stock.
Ricoeur, Paul (1991). 'The Model of the Text: Meaningful Action Considered as a Text.' In *From Text to Action: Essays in Hermeneutics II.* Trans. Kathleen Blamey and John B. Thompson. Evanston, IL: Northwestern University Press.
Ricoeur, Paul (1992). *Oneself as Another.* Trans. Kathleen Blamey. Chicago: University of Chicago Press.
Ricoeur, Paul, with Monique Canto-Serber (2004). 'Une laïcité d'exclusion est le meilleur ennemi de l'égalité.' *Le Monde diplomatique,* January.
Robinson, Ira (2007). *Rabbis and Their Community: Studies in the Immigrant Orthodox Rabbinate in Montreal, 1896–1930.* Calgary, AB: University of Calgary Press.
Robinson, Ira, ed. (1985). *Cyrus Adler: Selected Letters.* 2: 143–5. Philadelphia: Jewish Publication Society.
Robinson, Ira, and Mervin Butovsky, eds. (1995). *Renewing Our Days: Montreal Jews in the Twentieth Century.* Montréal: Véhicule.
Rocher, François, and Miriam Smith (2003). *New Trends in Canadian Federalism.* 2nd ed. Peterborough, ON: Broadview Press.
Roy, Olivier (2005). *La laïcité face à l'islam.* (*Secularism Confronts Islam,* 2007). Trans. George Holoch. New York: Columbia University Press. http://openpdf.com/ebook/olivier-roy-secularism-confronts-islam-pdf.html.
Ruby, Tabussum (2003). 'Immigrant Muslim Women and the Hijäb: Sites of Struggle in Crafting and Negotiating Identities in Canada.' MA thesis. University of Saskatchewan, Saskatoon.

Ryder, Bruce (2005). 'State Neutrality and Freedom of Conscience and Religion.' *Supreme Court Law Review* 29 (2): 174–9.
Saywell, John (2007). 'Mémoire.' Brief submitted to the Consultation Commission on Accommodation Practices Related to Cultural Differences. http://www.accommodements.qc.ca/documentation/memoires/St-Jerome/saywell-john-commission-de-consultation-sur-les-accommodements-raisonnables.pdf.
Schachter, Hindy Lauer (1993). 'Public School Teachers and Religiously Distinctive Dress: A Diversity-Centred Approach.' *Journal of Law and Education* 22: 61.
Schnoor, Randall (2002). 'Tradition and Innovation in an Ultra-Orthodox Community: The Hasidim of Outremont.' *Canadian Jewish Studies* 10: 53–73.
Scott, Joan Wallach (2007). *The Politics of the Veil*. Princeton, NJ: Princeton University Press.
Senior, Nancy (2007). 'The Muslim Headscarf Controversy in French Schools: A Sign of Inclusion or of Exclusion.' *Rhetor: Journal of the Canadian Society for the Study of Rhetoric* 2: 1–23. www.cssr-scer.ca/rhetor.
Smith, Adam (1759; 1790) *The Theory of Moral Sentiments*. 2 vols. 6th ed. London: W. Creech and J. Bell.
Sorensen, Jens Magleby (1996). *The Exclusive European Citizenship: The Case for Refugees and Immigrants in the European Union*. Aldershot, UK: Avebury.
Taylor, Charles (1985). *Social Theory as Practice*. Delhi: Oxford University Press.
Taylor, Charles (1991). *The Malaise of Modernity*. Concord, ON: House of Anansi Press.
Taylor, Charles (1992). *Multiculturalism and the 'Politics of Recognition': An Essay*. Princeton, NJ: Princeton University Press.
Taylor, Charles, James Tully, and Daniel M. Weinstock (1994). *Philosophy in an Age of Pluralism: The Philosophy of Charles Taylor in Question*. Cambridge: Cambridge University Press.
Thobani, Sunera (2007). *Exalted Subjects: Studies in the Making of Race and Nation in Canada*. Toronto: University of Toronto Press.
Tulchinsky, Gerald (1992). *Taking Root: The Origins of the Canadian Jewish Community*. Toronto: Lester Publishing.
Tulchinsky, Gerald (1998). *Branching Out: The Transformation of the Canadian Jewish Community*. Toronto: Stoddart.
Waller, Hall (2006). Canada. Philadelphia: American Jewish Committee.
Weil, Patrick (2009). 'Why the French Laïcité Is Liberal.' *Cardoza Law Review* 30 (6): 2700–14.
Weinfeld, Morton (2008). 'Québec Anti-Semitism and Anti-Semitism in Québec.' *Post Holocaust and Anti-Semitism* 64 (January): 1.

Winter, Bronwyn (2008). *Hijāb and the Republic: Uncovering the French Headscarf Debate*. Syracuse, NY: Syracuse University Press.

Woehrling, Jean-Marie (1998a). 'Réflexion sur le principe de neutralité de l'État en matière religieuse et sa mise en œuvre en droit français.' *Archives de Sciences Sociale des Religions* 101 (janvier-mars): 31–52.

Woehrling, José (1998b). 'L'obligation d'accommodement raisonnable et l'adaptation de la société à la diversité religieuse.' *McGill Law Journal* 43: 325–401.

Woehrling, José (2000). 'Convergences et divergences entre fédéralisme et protection des droits et libertés: L'exemple des États-Unis et du Canada.' *Revue de droit de McGill* 46: 21.

Woehrling, José (2009). 'Quelle place pour la religion dans les institutions publiques?' Dans *Le droit, la religion et le raisonnable: Le fait religieux entre monisme étatique et pluralisme juridique* (sous la direction de Jean-François Gaudreault-DesBiens), 115–68. Montréal: Éditions Thémis.